CLASSIFICATION FOR
INFORMATION RETRIEVAL

CLASSIFICATION FOR INFORMATION RETRIEVAL

PAPERS PRESENTED AT AN INTENSIVE COURSE HELD
IN SEPTEMBER 1967 AT THE SCHOOL OF LIBRARIANSHIP
LIVERPOOL COLLEGE OF COMMERCE

edited by K G B BAKEWELL FLA AMBIM

ARCHON BOOKS & CLIVE BINGLEY

CONTENTS

INTRODUCTION

THIS VOLUME CONTAINS the texts of six lectures delivered at an intensive course on classification for information retrieval held at the School of Librarianship, Liverpool College of Commerce, on September 19 and 20 1967. The idea for the course came from the chief librarian of a large industrial library in the Midlands who, after he and his senior staff had shown some of our students round his library, suggested that there was a need for schools of librarianship to organize ' crash ' courses to enable librarians working in industry to remain *au fait* with modern classification techniques. In view of this librarian's kind hospitality to our students, we felt that the least we could do was to test the demand for such a course, and the response was such that thirty representatives of twenty five organisations (mainly industrial firms) in various parts of Britain and Ireland visited Liverpool in September to hear these papers and to contribute to the discussions which they provoked.

All the lecturers were asked to compress as much information as possible into their hour-long talks while still leaving time for questions and discussion. This they did admirably, though some of the course participants may have suffered from mental indigestion by lunch-time on the second day, when the course closed. It is hoped that the publication of the proceedings will allow them to assimilate the information at their leisure as well as proving useful to other librarians/information officers, especially in industry, and to students of the Library Association examinations, notably B11 (Theory of classification), B12 (Theory of cataloguing), B31 (Handling and dissemination of information) and the list C papers concerned with the literature of science and technology.

Our aim was to marry theory and practice, especially on the first day when lectures by members of the full-time staff of Liverpool School of Librarianship on the Universal Decimal Classification (UDC) and faceted classification were each followed by talks on practical applications. This allowed the audience to hear what allegedly *could* happen and to compare this with what actually *did* happen. It was perhaps a good thing that the full-time students present, who welcomed the opportunity of hearing practising librarians talking about how *they* classified, should hear some of the theories advanced by their lecturers being ' hit for six ' as well as hearing others firmly supported.

7

The first morning was devoted to what might be termed 'traditional' classification, since UDC has been with us for almost the whole of the twentieth century. In his account of the use of UDC at Risley, Mr Thomas laid great stress on simplicity; but, as pointed out in the discussion, this means broad classification, and classification in depth can be vital in industry. The flexibility of UDC came in for criticism: can it be an international standard and still remain as flexible as it is? Is it not absolutely necessary to have a fixed citation order of symbols in order to achieve consistency in practice?

The afternoon of September 19 was devoted to the more modern ideas originally put forward by Dr Ranganathan. In a stimulating address at the end of the afternoon Mrs Jean Aitchison, who has probably had as much experience of 'facet' as any other English librarian, drew attention to some of the difficulties in its practical application. Mr Thomas had mentioned the value of chain indexing for collecting 'distributed relatives', but Mrs Aitchison showed, in no uncertain fashion, that chain indexing has its disadvantages. One of the other problems of specialised classification schemes is the need to provide for subjects outside the library's own special field, and one wondered whether this might not be an argument against gearing a classification scheme to a particular industry. Mrs Aitchison felt not: the ultimate solution might be the general faceted classification on which the Classification Research Group are at present engaged, but for the present one could make use of existing classifications in other fields—as some organisations were doing with the English Electric scheme.

One point which arose during Mr Maltby's lecture was whether scientists and technologists preferred faceted classification schemes to more traditional ones; Mrs Aitchison seemed doubtful about this, though some members of the audience thought it was so. The need for brief notations had been urged by Mr Thomas in his plea for simplicity when using UDC; during the discussion on Mr Maltby's paper, Mr Gomersall (English Electric Company) claimed that faceted classification could combine brevity of notation with classification in depth, supporting his argument by a comparison of notations for 'discoloration of copper' (620.191:669.3 in UDC, NCU Pg in the English Electric scheme). Mr Gomersall was also impressed by Mr Maltby's claim for the mnemonic value of faceted notations, pointing out that NCU could mean something to a metallurgist, since cu is the accepted symbol for copper, whereas 669.3 means nothing; brevity and mnemonics save scientists' time, said Mr Gomersall, and time means money. (In fairness it should be added that the UDC covers the whole of knowledge and the English Electric scheme covers an area of science and technology.)

Mrs Aitchison did not agree with a suggestion made during the discussion on her paper that co-ordinate indexing is preferable to faceted classification, since the former does not show relationships between subjects until the time of search. But this point, which was the last to be raised on the afternoon of September 19, was a good lead in to the proceedings of September 20, which might well have been labelled ' alternatives to classification '. Many librarians/information officers have been impressed by the apparent simplicity of co-ordinate indexing and want to know more. Few people are in a better position to tell them than Mr Johnson of British Insulated Callenders Cables Ltd, probably the pioneer of such systems in Britain. Drawing on his vast experience, Mr Johnson showed that, simple though co-ordinate indexing may be, there *are* snags, and some measure of classification is essential if the system is to work satisfactorily. Many of the snags are concerned with the compilation of the thesaurus, and it was problems of thesauri which occupied most of the discussion.

The course concluded with an interesting account by Mr Highcock of the use of KWOC (or, as he preferred to call it, KWAC) indexing at Unilever, whose techniques have been used as a model by at least one other firm in the north-west of England. A major problem with this system, emphasised during the discussion, is its reliance on titles; these are often ambiguous and may have to be amended by the indexer.

My thanks are due to all the speakers for sticking to their brief so admirably and for enabling me to pass their papers for publication with a minimum of delay; to my colleague Arthur Maltby for his invaluable help in organising the course and editing the proceedings; and to my wife for secretarial assistance. In conclusion, I should like to reiterate a point made by Mr Maltby during his closing remarks at the final discussion session. We at Liverpool School of Librarianship are very conscious of our duty to cater for the educational and training needs of *existing* information staff, especially in industry; for the past nine years we have organised an annual patents course, and the proceedings of a three-day symposium on *Information work today*, held in 1966, were published by Clive Bingley Ltd in 1967 under the editorship of Bernard Houghton. Dr D J Urquhart and others have stressed the desirability of short courses for industry, industry has shown that it will support such courses, and we shall go on providing them in so far as our commitments to our full-time students—obviously our prime responsibility—allow. We also invite any industrial librarians/information officers with problems concerning classification and indexing, to get in touch with us; if we cannot give you the answers, we may know somebody who can.

Woolton, Liverpool
October 1967

K G B BAKEWELL

THE UNIVERSAL DECIMAL CLASSIFICATION

K G B BAKEWELL FLA AMBIM
Lecturer, Liverpool School of Librarianship

THE UNIVERSAL DECIMAL CLASSIFICATION (UDC) had its origins in an abortive attempt to produce a card index of world literature following an international conference held in Brussels in 1895. Prime movers in this were two Belgians, Paul Otlet and Henri La Fontaine. The Institut de Bibliographie developed from the conference, and this body we now know as the Federation International de Documentation (FID). The card index was begun, but such a project, aiming to list books, documents and major periodical articles on all subjects and from all countries, was obviously doomed to failure. The card index eventually died, but UDC lives on to be the most widely used classification scheme in industrial libraries throughout the world.

The originators of the central index could have produced an entirely new classification scheme for the task they had in mind, or they could have chosen to adapt an existing scheme. In 1895 there was only one scheme which could reasonably be used as a basis, the Decimal classification of Melvil Dewey; the flexibility of Dewey's decimal notation and the international significance of arabic numbers made it ideal for the purposes envisaged, and it was adopted with Dewey's permission.

The first full edition was completed, in French, in 1905. There is, as yet, no complete English edition, though the third edition of an English abridgment was published in 1961[1]. Full expansions have appeared of most classes of interest to the industrial librarian, including the whole of pure science (though much of this is in urgent need of revision). Classes which have not yet been published in English include 621 mechanical engineering, 624/628 civil engineering, 65 management and 66 chemical engineering. A number of special subject editions have been published in English, including the Abridged Building Classification (ABC), issued by the International Council for Building Research in Rotterdam, the Special Subject edition for Metallurgy, issued by the Iron and Steel Institute as Special Report no 84, and the Special Subject Edition for Nuclear Science and Technology, sponsored jointly by the International Atomic Energy Agency and the United Kingdom Atomic Energy Authority.

It is worth bearing in mind that the word 'universal' has three meanings as applied to UDC: it is intended for all countries, embodies all knowledge, and, most important, allows any combination of concepts from any subject.

Dewey divided the whole of knowledge into nine sections, plus an additional section for generalia, as follows:

000 generalia
100 philosophy
200 religion
300 social sciences (including economics)
400 language
500 science
600 technology
700 fine arts
800 literature
900 history, travel, biography

Each 'hundred' was broken down into 'tens', the tens were further broken down by ten, and then decimal points were introduced after the third digit, as follows:

600 technology
620 engineering
621 mechanical engineering
621.9 machine tools

The use of decimals allows infinite flexibility: any new subject could be introduced between 621.8 and 621.9 merely by the addition of a digit.

UDC retained this basic order of subjects but abolished Dewey's 'three figure minimum' in notation, so that technology is now 6 and engineering 62. This has the double advantage of producing a shorter notation for general subjects and freeing some digits for expansion; thus, 620 could, if required, be used for a subdivision of engineering.

UDC retained this basic order of subjects but made a few adjustments which may prove a little confusing to the librarian who moves from Dewey to UDC. For example, welding is 671.52 in Dewey but 621.791 in UDC, and plastics is 668.4 in Dewey but 678.5 in UDC. One disadvantage of UDC for the industrial librarian is immediately apparent: only four of the classes (0, 3, 5 and 6) are really relevant to his needs, meaning that much of the notation is wasted.

But the most important alteration by far is the addition of a number of auxiliary signs and symbols, which increase the range of specification and also allow a considerable number of alternative arrangements to suit the needs of the particular library. The most useful of these signs is the colon, which indicates all kinds of relationship (*eg* comparison, influence or application); for example, 658:66 can mean management in the chemical industry, where 658 is industrial management and 66 is chemical technology; alternatively, this subject can be specified as 66:658. Whichever is used, one aspect must be 'hidden', and there are two ways of dealing with this problem; one is to make two entries in the classified catalogue, one under 658:66 and one under 66:658; the other, and more economical method, is to allow the subject index to bring out the hidden aspect, thus:

management   658
management: chemical industries 66:658

Square brackets are used to indicate subordinate relationships; for example, statistical analysis of production can be specified as 338[31], where 338 is production economics and 31 is statistics. A more valuable feature of square brackets is that they allow intercalation and enable a librarian to vary the 'official' order to suit his own particular needs. For example, 620.19 defects and deterioration in materials, may be divided by kind of defect (enumerated in the schedules) and by material (linking with another part of the tables), thus:

620.191   surface flaws and defects, discoloration
620.192   internal defects, swelling, shrinkage, etc
620.193   corrosion
620.191:669.3 discoloration of copper
620.191:669.4 discoloration of lead
620.192:669.3 swelling of copper
620.192:669.4 swelling of lead
620.193:669.3 corrosion of copper
620.193:669.4 corrosion of lead

This brings documents on corrosion, swelling, etc together, but information on materials is separated and can only be shown by the index or by added entries in the catalogue. If it is desired to have all material on defects of copper together, but at 620.19 rather than 669.3, this can be done by the use of square brackets, thus:

620.19[669.3]1 discoloration of copper
620.19[669.3]2 swelling of copper
620.19[669.3]3 corrosion of copper

or, if it is desired to keep every aspect of materials testing and defects of a material together:

620.1[669.3]91
620.1[669.3]92
620.1[669.3]93

Intercalation is not recommended in the UDC *Abridgment,* but it can be a very useful practice. It is stated in the *Abridgment* that (( )) can replace [ ] if a typewriter is being used.

The oblique stroke is used to link consecutive numbers as, for example, 534/536 heat, light and sound, where 534 is sound, 535 light and 536 heat, while the plus is used to join non-consecutive numbers so that a book dealing with both mining (622) and metallurgy (669) can be classified at 622+669. This last sign seems rather pointless: all that is needed is an added entry in the catalogue under the second number.

Language of a document can be specified, if necessary, by the equals sign, 624=30 denoting a book on civil engineering written in German. Parentheses are used to introduce both literary form and place; for example, 62(03) is an encyclopedia of engineering, 62(05) a periodical on engineering, 62(410) a document on engineering in England, and 62(73) a document on engineering in the United States. UDC provides numbers for general specification of place such as north, south, east and west, and also for physical place such as 'cold regions'. (1) indicates 'world' and can be very useful for indicating international coverage; the valuable *Patents throughout the world* by White and Ravenscroft can, for example, be classified at 608.7(1) and therefore kept separate from general treatises on patents. Period can be indicated by inverted commas: " 1967 " means quite simply, 1967, while " 196 " means in the 1960's and " 19 " means 'twentieth century'.

Various points of view of a subject can be brought together by using the 'point of view' numbers, which always begin with .00. I have previously stated that a book on 'management in the chemical industry' can be classified at 66:658; this is perfectly true, but often a more helpful order can be obtained by first using .008, the point of view number for management. For example, if 'Management in the electrical engineering industry' were specified as 621.3:658, this could file between, say, 621.3:63 electrical engineering *applied to agriculture,* and 621.3:69 electrical engineering *applied to building,* producing a not very helpful order; if, however, 'applications' are introduced by .002, 'practical point of view', and 'management aspects' are introduced by .008, a more helpful order results, thus:

621.3.002:63　electrical engineering in agriculture
621.3.002:69　electrical engineering for building
621.3.008:658　management in the electrical engineering industries.

The point of view numbers also include a number of common

subdivisions not applicable by (01/09), notably .001.5 research. Thus, 669.001.5 indicates 'research in the metallurgical industries'.

Race and nationality may be specified by (=0/=9), the numbers being taken from class 4 philology. For example, 'the employment of Arabs in engineering' may be specified as 62.007(=927), where 62 is engineering, .007 is the point of view number for personnel, and (=927) is Arabs.

All the auxiliaries mentioned so far may be applied to any subject, but there are three 'special auxiliaries', or SAN's, which are only applicable in certain classes. These are introduced by—, .0, and '. In the 62 class, for example, —52 always means 'automatic control' or 'automation', and at 629 transport engineering, .018 always means 'signalling equipment'. Some classifiers prefer 'colonning' to using SAN's, since they feel the latter hide information. For example, 629.12-52 automation in the shipbuilding industry, can only be given one place in the classified catalogue, but if 621-52 were colonned on to 629.12, two entries could be made and all aspects of automation collected at 621. However, as already stated when referring to colonning, the alphabetical index can be used to bring out the hidden aspects, thus:

automation	: aeronautical engineering	629.13-52
	: automobile engineering	629.2-52
	: shipbuilding	629.12-52
	: workshop practice	629.7-52
signalling	: aeronautical engineering	629.13.018
	: automobile engineering	629.2.018
	: shipbuilding	629.12.018

The apostrophe has more limited application, an example of its use being seen at 546 inorganic compounds where individual elements can be synthesised using ' to produce compounds. Thus, 546.621 is aluminium and 546.711 is manganese; therefore 546.621'711 is compounds of aluminium and manganese.

Finally, any subject may be further subdivided alphabetically. For example, 629.11 land and road vehicles, may be subdivided alphabetically by manufacturer producing:

629.11 British Motor Corporation

629.11 **Ford**

One important point about the auxiliaries is the tremendous flexibility which they allow, since no order is specified for their application, although there is a recommended order on page 10 of the British

Abridgment. Industrial relations in Great Britain in the twentieth century may, for example, be classified at 331.1"19"(410) (industrial relations—twentieth century—Great Britain), or 331.1(410)"19" (industrial relations—Great Britain—twentieth century), depending on whether the library wishes to collocate material on industrial relations of a particular period, or industrial relations of a particular country. More important, the auxiliaries of place and time lend themselves readily, like the square brackets sign, to intercalation, allowing even more variation according to the needs of each library. Using 331.1 again as an example, this is divided by such matters as labour contract (331.116), work regulations (331.14), arbitration (331.155) etc, but a library may well wish to keep everything relating to industrial relations in a particular country together and this can easily be done, thus:

331.1(410)	industrial relations in Great Britain
331.1(410)16	labour contract
331.1(410)4	work regulations
331.1(410)55	arbitration

FILING ORDER OF SYMBOLS

Since symbols have no ordinal value, they obviously have to be given a filing order, and this is stated on page 10 of the British *Abridgment*. It is as follows:

+	624+69	civil engineering and building
/	624/625	civil engineering including road and railway engineering
simple no	624	civil engineering
:	624:63	civil engineering in agriculture
[ ]	624[51]	mathematics in civil engineering
=	624=30	a document on civil engineering written in German
(01/09)	624(05)	a periodical on civil engineering
(1/9)	624(47)	civil engineering in the USSR
(=)	624(=927)	Arabs in civil engineering
" "	624"19"	civil engineering in the twentieth century
A/Z (alphabetical subdivision)	624 Taylor Woodrow	a document on the activities of Taylor Woodrow in the field of civil engineering
.00	624.003	civil engineering from the economic point of view

| — | 624—78 | safety in civil engineering |
| .0 | 624.05 | site organization |

The apostrophe, when used, files after the dash.

It is stated that period divisions may, if preferred, be filed before place divisions. There are, however, at least two other desirable changes: the language sign should surely follow the simple number, since at present a general book on civil engineering will *follow* a book on a more specific aspect simply because it happens to be written in a foreign language; more important, a German book on civil engineering may be separated from the same book in English for which, in an English library, the language may not have been specified. The other major fault is that / should precede +, since the former is more general; better still, as previously stated, not to use + at all, but to give an added entry in the catalogue under the second number.

It should be emphasised that this is a *filing* order and not an order of *citation* of symbols. As previously stated, the latter is left to the discretion of each individual library, although a recommended order is given.

USE OF UDC

UDC was, as stated, originally intended for the classification of a card index of world literature. It now aims to be an international standard classification, and it is no accident that the responsibility for its production and marketing in several countries lies with the national standards organisation. In Britain it is issued by the British Standards Institution as British Standard 1000. Its use in Russia for scientific and technical literature has been compulsory since 1963. It has never been popular in the United States, but the position may be changing: the National Federation of Science Abstracting and Indexing Services' *A guide to the world's abstracting and indexing services in science and technology* (1963), prepared by the Library of Congress under a grant from the National Science Foundation, includes a list of abstracting services arranged according to the UDC. In Britain the trend seems, in industrial libraries at any rate, to be away from UDC in favour of faceted classifications or co-ordinate indexing.

A second important use of UDC is for what Dr S R Ranganathan has called 'pre-natal classification'. Many documents and periodical articles now appear with a ready-made class number, thus saving the librarian a great deal of time and trouble—provided he agrees with the class number! Most national standards are issued with a UDC number and UDC is used as the basis of a number of abstracting journals such as *World fisheries abstracts* and *Electrical and electronics abstracts*. In Britain, the Cement and Concrete Association usually gives a UDC number to its reports and *Engineering* classifies the very useful ' Outlines ' which it began about two years ago by UDC. Journals which classify their articles by UDC include *Russian journal of inorganic chemistry, AEI engineering, the Post Office electrical engineers' journal, Stal, Bautechnik, Materialprüfung* and many others.

REVISION

UDC's revision method is both a strength and a weakness; it is certainly democratic, but it is also slow. Any UDC user may submit proposals for revision through the appropriate national body, which forwards them to the Central Classification Committee (CCC), the FID body responsible for the development and maintenance of UDC. If approved by the CCC, each proposal is circulated to subscribers as a ' P note ', and if no objection is forthcoming the change is published in *Extensions and corrections to the UDC*, which is issued twice a year.

Generally speaking, UDC numbers may be *extended* or *restricted*, but not completely altered. If a number becomes obsolete it may be cancelled and eventually used again, but only after it has been ' frozen ' for ten years, which is considered the minimum period necessary to enable current users to readjust their files and to avoid widespread confusion of the older and the newer meanings. An example at the moment is that class 4 philology is being moved to class 8 literature; at the end of its ten-year period, it could be used to extend the overcrowded 5 and 6 classes. Two suggestions made for doing this are *a*) using 4 as a bridge between 3 social sciences and 5 science, with places for techno-commercial subjects such as information processing, communication and control, and management; or *b*) linking scientific phenomena and applications[2]. Either of these changes would result in a very different UDC from the one we know today.

CONCLUSIONS

UDC has much to commend it to the industrial librarian seeking an efficient classification scheme. It covers the whole of knowledge, and this can be a very useful feature, since all industrial libraries have to collect material way outside their own particular subject field; its notation is fairly easy to follow and of international significance; as an international standard, it can form the basis of co-operation in various bibliographical activities—though if it is really to act as a standard, an approved citation order of symbols must be adhered to and it will then lose some of its flexibility; its notation could form the basis of a computer language; and it has permanent machinery for maintenance. But this machinery can be slow, and there are also other faults. It is built on an obsolete and unscientific framework. It perpetuates Dewey's separation of science and technology, 54 chemistry and 66 chemical technology being widely separated, for example. It distributes aspects of a subject according to their major relationship—coal, for example, being found at chemical technology (662.66 and 662.74), geology (553.9) and mining (622.33); this is inevitable in general libraries, but it is not always helpful for special libraries. The notation can be complex, especially if many of the auxiliary symbols are used at once; also, there is an excessive notational burden laid on the 5 and 6 classes, science and technology; Lloyd has pointed out that seventy-two percent of the total space of the schedules is used by these two classes[2]. There is no full English edition as yet, and there is delay in producing new editions, which are sadly needed in several areas.

Vickery has summed up the situation very neatly: ' its size and universality will not save UDC if it is unable to advance with science and technology '[3].

REFERENCES
1 *Universal decimal classification: abridged English edition.* London, British Standards Institution, third edition 1961 (British Standard 1000A; 1961).
2 Lloyd, G A: ' Science and technology in the future UDC revision ' *Revue internationale de la documentation,* 30 (4) November 1963, pp 132-7.
3 Vickery, B C: ' The universal decimal classification and technical information indexing ' UNESCO *Bulletin for libraries,* 15 (3) May-June 1961, pp 126-38 and 147.

OTHER READINGS
British Standards Institution: *Guide to the universal decimal classification* [by J Mills]. London, British Standards Institution, 1963 (British Standard 1000C: 1963).

Mills, J: *The universal decimal classification.* New Brunswick (NJ), Rutgers University Press, 1964. (Rutgers University Graduate School of Library service, Rutgers series on systems for the intellectual organization of information, volume 1).

Schuchmann, M: ' The universal decimal classification: yesterday, today and tomorrow ' (*in Classification research: proceedings of the Second International Study Conference held at Hotel Prins Hamlet, Elsinore, Denmark, 14th to 18 September 1964.* Copenhagen, Munksgaard, 1965).

PRACTICAL APPLICATION OF UDC

J R THOMAS
Information Officer, United Kingdom Atomic Energy Authority, Risley

THE CLASSIFIER AT his desk has to face numerous problems which do not arise in a theoretical consideration of the classification scheme. He will probably have only a limited knowledge of the subjects of the documents with which he is dealing. He will often have to deal with articles with ill-defined subject content and misleading titles. The classification schedules contain many ambiguities and are open to considerable misinterpretation. Subjects are not clearly defined fields, as represented by a Boolean diagram, but diffuse, shading one into another.

This lecture is based on experience at the Atomic Energy Authority over a number of years. UDC is applied to some 4,000 reports per annum, and classification is carried out in four different establishments; copies of the union catalogue are held throughout the authority.

Mr Bakewell referred to the various meanings of 'universal' as applied to UDC. One meaning it obviously does not have is 'invariable'; classifiers in Liverpool and Washington are unlikely to produce the same number for a given document. In fact, UDC is almost too flexible, making the attainment of consistency very difficult. The mind boggles at the fun which could be produced by the circulation of a postcard message written in UDC symbols.

In applying UDC there are two primary considerations: the number and type of items to be classified, and the type of enquiry to be answered. The use of UDC demands considerable intellectual effort at the input stage, so it is certainly inappropriate for ephemeral material. Also, it would seem a waste of time and effort to use it for documents which are going to be covered by one of the published abstracting services.

The great problem in practical application is how to achieve consistency. It has been said that it does not matter if one uses a wrong number, provided one uses it consistently—an exaggerated statement, but one with some truth in it. The keynote in maintaining consistency, particularly bearing in mind the tremendous flexibility previously referred to, is simplicity, and this means restricted subdivision. The depth of classification can be restricted in accordance with the number of documents to be classified and the breadth of enquiries to be answered. For example, consider the following array of catalogue entries, each number having only one document classified at it:

---

* (*Mr Thomas' paper is here reported by the Editor.*)

535.1
535.214.4
535.215:537.311
535.215.08:551.574.1
535.24

It would obviously be simpler to stop at the sixth digit, thus avoiding complications in filing and retrieval, and the order of the entries would be virtually unaltered. A useful rule would be to restrict subdivision of any number until it had been used for the classification of at least twenty documents. Also, if the breadth or vagueness of the majority of enquiries were such as to require the scanning of, say, two hundred entries under a particular class mark, then there would seem to be no point in fine subdivision. The more detailed the classification, the more difficult it becomes to ensure consistency and to co-ordinate the work of different classifiers.

The process of classifying involves two steps, identifying the subject matter and assigning the class number. It has been argued that the second process is a clerical one, but it is difficult to separate the two. Subject identification is an intellectual operation which demands a certain amount of subject knowledge and, in particular, the ability to assess the subject content and to extract what is ' news ' as distinct from background information. For example, a document on *the design of scrubbing towers for the manufacture of sulphuric acid* might quote the chemical reactions involved, but this information would be irrelevant from a classification point of view; interest would be centred on the aspect which is ' news ', the engineering design. A document may also contain useful information unrelated to the main subject, and this information must be identified for classification.

One approach (the single entry or permuted single entry method) is to identify the primary subject, and this is naturally applicable when dealing with books for shelving purposes. It is liable to produce notations of inordinate length, particularly when applied to report literature, and an unhelpful order in the classified file.

A second approach (the multiple entry method) avoids the difficult problem of the identification of the primary subject. The schedules are considered as an array of concepts: the main classes, for example, are equivalent to major disciplines of learning and the subclasses (' tens ') represent textbook treatment of a subject. When classifying, one considers ' in relation to which concepts will this document be of interest?', and makes an entry for each one. A document on *spray nozzles for cooling towers,* for example, may be required both for the information it contains on spray nozzles and for that on cooling towers, so that the two entries are needed.

Subdivision may be restricted according to the number of entries expected in a particular field, and consistency can be achieved by restricting subdivision to the facets giving the most useful array. The common names of some nuclear reactors are illustrative. The names ' Magnox ', 'Advanced gas-cooled' and ' Steam generating heavy water ' suggest that the designers considered the primary aspect of each design to be based on a different characteristic in each case:

Magnox fuel element cans (*ie* can material)

Gas cooled (*ie* coolant)

Heavy water moderated boiling water cooled (*ie* moderator + coolant). To use aspects such as these for the subdivision of reactor designs would result in chaos, and in the Atomic Energy Authority subdivision is restricted to the facets indicated in the third example, moderator + coolant.

Objections to the multiple entry method are that one is left without a primary number for shelving purposes and that a bulky catalogue will be produced.

The relationship between the two approaches and the methods of making entries may be very roughly represented as follows:

A : B : C   single entry

A : B : C
B : C : A   permuted (cycled) single entry
C : A : B

A
B   multiple entry
C

Satisfactory classification only comes with a good knowledge of the schedules, and this knowledge can only be gained by ' learning ' them with use. Apart from the problem of when to use a colon and when an auxiliary, the classifier will meet many other difficulties in his daily work. Not the least is the lack of a schedule of materials as such. Numbers for specific materials occur in several of the main classes, which is to be expected as chemists, chemical engineers and metallurgists are all very interested in materials. On the other hand, classifiers may have a legitimate desire to collect together information on a particular material, and they must then decide which of the schedules containing subdivisions for materials they will use. As an example one may consider a document on *the electrical conductivity of copper.* Classically, one must presumably place this at 537.311.31 as the subject is physics; in using instead 546.56 (chemistry of copper) or 669.3 (metallurgy of copper) one is extending the meaning of those schedules.

There may be a choice of alternative characteristics, as for example at 669.1 iron & steel:

669.14.018 steels by properties
669.141   steels by methods of production
669.15   steels by composition

Without having made a prior decision, a classifier would be likely to obtain an unhelpful array by placing stainless steel under 669.14.018, a mild steel under 669.141, and a nickel-chromium steel under 669.15. Documents such as progress reports of establishments and reports of visits in which the subject is usually diffuse can only be classified at more general numbers, but for many purposes collections under the subdivisions of form are found useful.

In the specialised field of a collection, subjects may be encountered which appear very complex. A document on the behaviour of AGR fuel elements will have at least five aspects of interest from a retrieval point of view: reactor type, fuel elements, uranium dioxide fuel, stainless steel canned fuel, behaviour in service. A single entry for such a document would need to be unreasonably long, but by making separate entries (three in the Authority) collections can be provided to enable retrieval of the document from any aspect of interest.

Individual methods of chemical analysis often cause difficulty, since the 543 schedule does not provide the subdivisions to answer the commonest information request. An analyst is usually searching for methods of determination of a substance or the analysis of a material, and not for the applications of an analytical method such as absorptiometry. A document on *the gasometric determination of carbon in steel* is likely to be required primarily from the points of view of the determination of carbon and the analysis of steel.

The classifier can only solve these problems by carefully examining the schedules and coming to his own conclusions. He will often find that, for his own special field, he will require more subdivision than is enumerated, and this must be achieved by selective use of the auxiliary signs and the colon. He may be able to make ' unofficial ' adjustments in order to reduce the length of the notation; in the Atomic Energy Authority, for example, 621.039 is replaced by N for nuclear reactors.

In the Authority the principles enumerated above, and the corresponding decisions which have to be made and adhered to are contained in a code of practice. This code restricts the degree of subdivision of main numbers which may be used, specifies the permitted subdivision by colon and auxiliary, and establishes the citation order.

An alphabetical subject index is vital as a key to the numbers actually used, and this may be either a chain index or a natural language index. The great value of chain indexing is that it automatically collects aspects of a subject which are scattered in the schedules; a disadvantage is the difficulty often found in its use. In the absence of a code of practice the index helps to achieve consistency, and this is further assisted by the maintenance of an authority file in which are recorded all local decisions, such as when to use auxiliaries and their citation order.

As has been emphasised, consistency can only be expected if simplicity is practised: the inexperienced classifier should repress his desire to classify in great depth and remember that there is much virtue in short numbers.

FACETED CLASSIFICATION

A MALTBY BA FLA
Senior Lecturer, Liverpool School of Librarianship

FACETED CLASSIFICATION IS basically an attempt to act upon the realisation that most subjects are compounds, made up of two or more basic elements, and that if a classification recognises and lists these fundamental elements, providing also rules for their assembly, it has no need to enumerate the compound subjects. A fully faceted system divides its subject field (or, if it is a general system, each subject field) into categories or facets and each category consists of the elements produced by a single characteristic of division. The traditional approach to library classification was to list the subjects themselves along with their class-marks, rather than to identify and enumerate once and for all basic recurring elements. The state of modern knowledge is so complex and so subject to change, that the rigid listing of topics in a single vast hierarchy has great difficulty in coping with it. In the special library, more than elsewhere, there is a need for a flexible system which allows concepts to be freely combined, and there are now available a number of special classifications which list basic elements in their appropriate facets and fully recognise the need for synthesis—that is, to arrive at a class-mark by fitting together symbols representing the elements involved in any compound theme. Each of these elements comes from a particular facet comprising a list of homogeneous concepts from the subject field. The older library classifications which cover knowledge in its totality are said to be enumerative rather than synthetic, because they usually try (all too often in vain) to list every subject in a systematic—general to special—hierarchy, and to provide each subject with a ready made class-mark.

A fully synthetic, or faceted, classification relies on the fitting together of elements from facets, the combination order of these elements being based on the needs of specialists in the subject field, so that a helpful sequence of documents, or of cards in a classified information index is promoted. If, for example, we have to cope with subjects such as 'advertising in the USA in 1967' or 'the tanning of leather', the enumerative scheme will seek to list the subjects concerned. The faceted classification, however, will piece together appropriate elements from the materials and operations facets in the case of the latter example, while the other subject will be dealt with by the linking together of an element from the activities facet of the commerce schedule, and elements from the common geographical and time facets in this order. It is clear that the approach of a faceted scheme is obviously akin to that of UDC, but the latter system has grafted its synthetic features on to the enumerative framework of the Dewey decimal classification, rather than beginning anew and creating a classification that was entirely faceted.

Why might an information officer or a special librarian want to use a fully faceted scheme? It can be argued that shelf arrangement of documents has rather a small part to play in the plans of many special libraries, since relatively little of the literature is in book form, and it is sometimes said too that, as no classification can collect all related material, the operation is a time-consuming and wasteful one. The first of these remarks deserves some attention, although there are not many special libraries where the post co-ordination of concepts through an indexing system can entirely replace classification in the usual sense. In most cases the co-ordinate indexing of report literature is complementary to the classification of books and a classified catalogue; indeed co-ordinate indexing itself, while rejecting notation, makes a good deal of use of classificatory principles in the structuring of the vocabulary for its thesaurus and in its use of linking devices. The other statement—arguing for the abolition of classification—is some-times advanced by those who should know better. It is surely a retro-gressive policy to abandon the attempt to show subject groupings in a catalogue or on the shelves simply because *all* groupings cannot be shown! What is wanted, of course, is a flexible system which will enable us to reveal major relationships in a sequence of documents or in a catalogue/information file, and a fully faceted system greatly aids the accomplishment of this task.

There are a number of reasons that can be advanced to support the last statement, one being that the possibility of synthesis through the linking together of elements provides the necessary detail for accurate classing at the documentation level. It is virtually impossible to enume-rate all the compound themes with which the special librarian has to contend, but they can be economically specified through the synthetic approach. If some of this detail is not required, it need not be employed but, to stress a point which J Mills has often made, it should be there for the library that wants it. A modern faceted scheme can, in addi-tion to dealing with compound themes, also cope with what we now call complex documents—these dealing not with elements from a single field of knowledge but rather with the impact of one field upon another—by the use of Ranganathan's technique of phase analysis All the detail is achieved without resorting to bulky classification schedules. Every recurring element is listed once only within its

34

appropriate facet, thus avoiding the tedious repetition of fundamental concepts that is found in the older, enumerative schemes. The fact that the classification schedules are slim undoubtedly makes them simpler to consult, and it is almost certainly easier to construct a faceted special scheme than to try to identify all the compound topics that may crop up within the specialised field, and then to try to list these in a helpful order. It has also been claimed that the library user, especially if he is a scientist or an engineer, finds a faceted classification more intelligible than an enumerative system.

The faceted schemes, like others, need revision at times but they are able to keep pace more readily with advances in the field of knowledge than enumerative classifications possibly can. Many ' new ' subjects are, in reality, found to involve merely a fresh combination of elements which a faceted scheme has already identified and listed within appropriate categories. Another asset is that the notation of such a scheme is likely to have a high mnemonic value, for each recurring element is constantly represented by the same symbol or symbols, and one can readily carry in the mind the class-mark of a heavily utilised concept. Above all, however, in making a claim for the employment of a faceted classification in special libraries, I wish to emphasise in some detail the flexibility of such systems and the way in which they can clarify the principles at stake for the achievement of helpful order.

Flexibility is seen in the removal of what we might call the ' unwanted intermediaries ' of classification. Consider the following example, where an imaginary but typical extract from the hierarchy of an enumerative classification is shown :

P   plastics
PB   vinyl plastics and resins
PBA   vinyl plastics as adhesives
PC   polystyrenes
PCJ   extrusion of polystyrenes
PCT   use of polystyrenes for wall tiles
PD   polyester resins
PDL   use of polyesters as protective coatings
PE   epoxy resins
PEL   use of epoxy resins for road repairs
        etc

It is clear that, while the hierarchy may be the most useful one, it is merely a single example of several hierarchies that could be enumerated from this subject field and many combinations of elements are effectively 'shut out'. In our hierarchy here, we can cope with *vinyl plastics* and *vinyl plastics as adhesives* but not with *plastics as adhesives* —vinyl crops up as an unwanted intermediary with regard to the last example. Nor can we classify readily topics such as *the extrusion of vinyl resins* or *vinyl plastics for wall tiles* unless recurring themes are inserted into the tables at virtually every point! Let us now examine the situation in a similar extract from a faceted scheme in which, for convenience, each facet has been allotted a distinctive form of notation:

Class P plastics

Facets:	Types	Forms	Processes	Applications
	A vinyl plastics	a adhesives	1 calendering	01 wall tiles
	B polystyrenes	b coatings	2 casting	02 pipe linings
	C polyesters	c films, sheets	3 extrusion	03 phonograph records
	D epoxies etc	d synthetic fibres etc	4 coating	
			5 laminating	04 road repairs etc

Here we know that, if the combination (or citation) order of facets is types, forms, processes, applications, then *vinyl plastics* will be PA and *vinyl plastics as adhesives* PAa. But if the types facet is not represented, combination can still take place—thus *plastics as adhesives* can be specified as Pa. In this way the rigidity of enumerative classification is largely removed. There is, it is true, an established order of facet combination but, if one facet is not represented, the others combine in their usual sequence. So *vinyl plastics for wall tiles* is PA01 and *extrusion of plastics* goes at P3. All compound themes can be handled in the system without recourse to the constant repetition of the basic concepts or elements. It may be objected that several elements in the applications facet only relate to one or two elements in the types facet. This is really an instance of differential facets—a problem which the advanced reader of classification should study.

All this detail and ability to classify precisely is vain unless helpful order is achieved, and it is necessary to substantiate the claim made above that a faceted system elucidates the principles for obtaining helpful order. A useful sequence of documents or catalogue entries through the use of a faceted scheme must depend upon *a*) the combination order of facets; and *b*) the order in which elements are listed within each facet.

The first of these is probably the most vital. The facet that is most concrete, or of major significance, must come first in the combination order and the others must be cited in a sequence of diminishing importance, or decreasing concreteness. Thus, in the example given in this paper, it is argued that it is better to keep together information regarding a particular type of plastic and to have some scattering of material concerning, say, a certain application than vice versa. Ranganathan has tried to link the idea of decreasing concreteness to the quasimetaphysical formula 'Personality, Matter, Energy, Space and Time', but this has given rise to some problems, and most special librarians making a suitable faceted classification would probably prefer to work out a citation order of facets for their own subject field in the light of an examination of some representative documents, and with regard to the typical demands for information that are received. It is possible that some specialist help in this respect can be drawn from some of the library's users. Likewise an attempt must be made, with or without aid from subject experts, to find a systematic principle to govern the order of listing the array of co-ordinate elements that are found within each facet.

When these two points governing helpful order have been carefully settled, it will be found necessary to file the individual facets in the exact reverse of their order of combination. This idea, usually referred to as the principle of inversion, seems odd at first glance but it ensures that everything on the primary facets is kept together, as can be demonstrated from seeing the order in which documents would appear in the theoretical system for *plastics* outlined above:

P	plastics
PO1	plastics for wall tiles
P3	extrusion of plastics
Pa	plastics as adhesives
PA	vinyl plastics
PAO1	vinyl plastics for wall tiles
PA3	extrusion of vinyl plastics
PAa	vinyl plastics as adhesives
	etc

Here, all documents relating to vinyl plastics have been collected through employment of the idea of *filing* the secondary facets before the primary ones. Scattering is thus confined to the minor facets—to applications and, to a lesser extent, to processes and forms. We are, therefore, readily able to determine what material has been kept together in the scheme and what has been separated, and we know that the latter will relate to the least concrete facets. With this knowledge, we can set out to ensure that the classification's alphabetical subject index (and that of our classified catalogue) complements rather than repeats the subject arrangement favoured by the classification itself. The customary way to achieve this support for the classification is through the use of a technique known as chain indexing. This involves examining the elements of a compound subject and indexing them in a specific-to-general order—the reverse of their order of citation in the classification. Thus in the index we would find entries such as:

adhesives: plastics	Pa
adhesives: vinyl plastics	PAa

or

wall tiles: plastics (in general)	POI
wall tiles: polystyrenes	PBOI
wall tiles: vinyl plastics	PAOI

and so forth. Many of the comparatively minor subject relationships which the classification has been obliged to ignore can be brought out in the alphabetical index through this method of making the indexing process reveal the various contexts in which specific themes can appear. Chain indexing is intended as an economical method of revealing in the index those approaches to the subject field which the classification has necessarily rejected. It has been argued that the chain procedure allows this to be done without calling upon the index to show *all* the possible combinations of elements. Nevertheless, in some subject fields, it may be objected that the classification and the index based on the chain procedure do not cater between them for all possible subject searches; in these circumstances the answer seems to be the use of the ' rotated ' index where each element is brought to the fore in turn. Such an index has been well described in the introduction to D J Foskett's *London education classification*[1], an excellent example of the fully faceted system. Yet, whatever method of indexing is employed, it is clear that the major groupings should be revealed by the classification itself and it must be reiterated that, in a faceted scheme, the factors involving this achievement of helpful order emerge more clearly than in the classifications based on the traditional idea of enumeration.

Nowadays co-ordinate indexing and mechanised systems for the retrieval of information are also making a great impact upon special librarianship and we shall hear something of them in later papers. The great advantage of co-ordinate indexing lies in the fact that concepts are only combined at the time of search, and its great problem lies in the construction of a suitable indexing vocabulary where, as has already been stated, the principles of classification are often required. One can only add that, if a faceted classification is used for arrangement on the shelves, and for a classified catalogue of a special library's bookstock, while technical reports are organised through co-ordinate indexing, the concepts or elements of the faceted scheme greatly aid the construction of the thesaurus for the indexing system. A faceted scheme is also well equipped to be used in conjunction with computer searching or a similar mechanised programme.

Some of these arguments in favour of classification through facet analysis can, no doubt, seem over-theoretical when a librarian is faced with the problem of constructing one, but in dealing with the *Why?* of faceted classification I hope I have given a brief indication of the *How?* also, and this is dealt with more fully in Vickery's book, *Faceted classification: a guide to the making and use of special schemes*[2]. Certainly a careful appraisal of the subject field is needed to determine what are the facets and which ones must be regarded as the primary, or most concrete, ones. That such schemes can be successfully constructed is attested by the number of special faceted classifications made in Britain in recent years and, if experience dictates that alterations to the scheme are required, it is certainly easier to adjust a system of this type than one which presents us with an almost interminable hierarchy of compound subjects in general to special order.

It is difficult, as Shakespeare pointed out, to turn the accomplishment of many years into an hour glass, and certainly this rapid survey of faceted classification has leaned heavily on the accomplishment and pioneering work of others over many years. In concluding, it is worthwhile to contrast the fully faceted approach briefly with that of the Universal decimal classification although, to follow one Shakespearean quotation almost immediately with an adaptation of another, I am here to praise faceted classification—not to try to bury UDC! It does appear that, for the British industrial librarian, UDC has advantages over a special system based on the analysis of a single subject field into its facets, in that UDC is a widely accepted standard which is used by many technical journals and abstracting services, and which promotes uniformity of practice. In addition, it covers all knowledge and thus copes with ' fringe ' material, as well as the library's major field of interest, and it is readily available, while a faceted classification may have to be constructed from scratch. Yet a faceted scheme fully utilises the great advantages of synthetic classification, whereas UDC still partly reflects the DC framework, with its weaknesses in order and faulty groupings and, if a faceted scheme has to be specially made, it should result in a system that is really geared to the needs of the library and information service concerned. Above all, the principles behind the fully faceted classification provide detail with helpful order. In contrast to this, the failure of UDC to recognise fully the principle of inversion, or to give a definite standard filing order to its many auxiliary tables for synthesis, means that its claims to promote uniformity of practice are weakened, and that detail is often only achieved at the expense of an arrangement of the maximum helpfulness in the classified information file. Efficiency must surely be prized more highly than availability or standardisation. This is not to say that UDC is inefficient; far from it. But a well constructed faceted classification can utilise fully certain principles which were only imperfectly grasped by librarians in the days when UDC was initiated and developed, and the faceted system is thus likely to be the more efficient tool. My own opinion—and this final sentence is no more than that—is that expediency will favour the use of UDC in special libraries, but that the continuing expansion of science and technology and the demand for efficiency in information work will dictate the making of classifications and indexing systems which fully put to use the knowledge and experience that is available to the modern librarian confronted with the problem of organising his materials.

REFERENCES

[1] Foskett, D J: *The London education classification.* London University Institute of Education, 1964 (*Education libraries bulletin,* supplement 6). (The introduction to this contains a splendid short account of the value of the faceted approach.)

[2] Vickery, B C: *Faceted classification: a guide to the making and use of special schemes.* London, ASLIB, 1960.

OTHER READINGS ON FACETED CLASSIFICATION

Foskett, D J: 'The construction of a faceted classification for a special subject' (*in Science, humanism and libraries.* London, Crosby Lockwood, 1964, pp 143-165).

Vickery, B C: *Faceted classification schemes.* New Brunswick (NJ), Rutgers University Press, 1966, (Rutgers University Graduate School of Library Service, Rutgers series on systems for the intellectual organization of information volume 5).

A list of special schemes of a faceted character appears in Vickery, B C: *Classification and indexing in science.* London, Butterworth, second edition 1959.

Foskett, D J: 'Classification' (*in* Ashworth, Wilfred, *ed Handbook of special librarianship and information work*. London, ASLIB, third edition 1967, chapter 4).

Mills, J: *Modern outline of library classification*. London, Chapman & Hall, 1960, chapter 13.

Sayers, W C Berwick: *Manual of classification*. London, Deutsch, fourth edition revised by A Maltby 1967, chapter 24.

PRACTICAL APPLICATION OF FACET CLASSIFICATION

with special reference to the English Electric Faceted Classification for Engineering

JEAN AITCHISON BA FLA
Formerly Chief Librarian, Central Library English Electric Company Ltd

Facet techniques have been used to construct a number of special classification schemes for subjects ranging from diamond technology to education, and from aeronautics to music. The English Electric *Faceted classification for engineering* is one such scheme. It was first published in 1958 and has been in use in the English Electric central and other libraries for the past seven years. This facet scheme is a particularly useful illustration of the practical application of facet principles, since not only has it been used to classify a large manual catalogue but it has survived a long period of full-scale operation. A study of the operating difficulties and successes with this scheme should give some indication of the performance of the average facet classification scheme.

The third edition of the English Electric *Faceted classification for engineering* appeared in 1961[1]. This is the scheme now in use in the English Electric libraries; but considerable amendments and additions have been made to the schedules over the years. Now a fourth edition is being compiled and should be published next year. In this paper both the old and the forthcoming editions of the schedules are considered.

B. FACET CHARACTERISTICS

Like all facet schemes, the English Electric classification can be distinguished by its ' analytico-synthetic nature '. It is analytical in so far as it examines thoroughly the nature of concepts and terms and sorts them into homogeneous groups according to well-defined characteristics. It is synthetic because, in it, concepts are isolated in such a way that they are free to combine with one another to express complex phrases and themes.

B.I. ANALYTICAL CHARACTERISTICS—B.I.I. *Analytical characteristics of detailed schedules:* Facet schemes should show simplicity and clarity in the arrangement of detailed schedules. This is true of the best of the tables in the English Electric schedules. Here facet scores by being able to give logical and concise arrangements of concepts in complex subject fields. Concepts are sorted into groups, and before each new group of concepts the characteristic of division is clearly stated (see table 1A).

In some schedules the layout is slightly different, the statement concerning the characteristic of division being replaced by a generic heading with its own notation followed by its species (see table 1B).

In some subject fields it is not easy to discern clear cut characteristics; when this occurs, provided the number of concepts in the field is small, it is sometimes preferable to leave the terms in alphabetical order. The example for capacitors (table 1C) is taken from the draft fourth edition schedules. Here the characteristics ' by purpose ' and ' by mode of construction ' have been recognised; but since a number of the types of capacitors included in the schedule could be classified under both of these categories, alphabetical order might be the best solution unless more helpful characteristics of division can be found.

It should be stressed that the analytical decisions made for a subject field are not immutable. Facet analysis is a tool which may assist in giving a helpful—and occasionally an illuminating—map of the subject field; but the arrangement which results will certainly not be the only way of arranging that field by facet analysis. The analysis can be only as good as the technical knowledge and analytical skill of the documentalist. Like any classification or thesaurus, it will fall out of date as new knowledge accumulates, and frequent additions and revisions are necessary. After seven years the English Electric libraries are finding that even the better-constructed tables (for mechanical engineering, heavy electrical engineering) are out-of-date and revised characteristics of division will be needed in the new edition.

B.1.2. *Analytical errors in the framework of the scheme:* At the time when the scheme was developed, the accepted method of making a faceted classification was, first, to define the area of knowledge to be covered, and then to use facet analysis to identify the ' fundamental concepts ' discernible in that field. This was done for the English Electric scheme; but the analytical decisions which were reached included two major errors from which the third edition has suffered ever since. The field to be classified was defined as ' the products of the English Electric and associated companies and the supporting processes of research, development and production '. This first decision was a mistaken one. The field to be classified should have been engineering as a whole, without a bias towards the interests of a particular company. It should have been obvious that the interests of a large concern are neither static nor limited to those fields immediately concerned with its main products. It is intended to remedy this defect in the fourth edition and to treat engineering from a general and unbiased viewpoint.

The second analytical error was to treat the whole area of engineering as if it were a small, compact, highly-specialised subject field, such as soil science or librarianship, and to divide it by 'fundamental categories', namely into the categories of 'personality', 'matter', 'energy' and 'space', derived from the PMEST formula of Ranganathan (see table 2).

It will be seen that the traditional academic subject divisions have been ignored in the arrangement of primary facets, and this has caused many irritating anomalies. For example, there is no place in the schedules for the recognised disciplines of electrical, mechanical or hydraulic engineering as such, since their constituent parts are scattered across the primary categories. Electrical components at H are separated from electrical machines at B, mechanical machines at D are separated from mechanical components at J/K. Other subjects, such as management, for example, are classified in one category (operation) and logically should not (although they do) contain personality and property concepts. The artificiality of the framework of the scheme is most apparent when the classification is used to arrange books on the shelves, or for broad subject divisions in reading lists, information bulletins and other library publications. Fortunately, defects in the overall structure are less obvious in 'depth indexing', where the effectiveness of the analysis within the detailed schedules is the major influence. Plans are being made for a return to the traditional divisions of engineering in the fourth edition with analysis of 'fundamental categories' within and not across these 'canonical' divisions (see table 3).

B. 2. SYNTHETIC CHARACTERISTICS: D J Foskett, in the introduction to his *London education classification*[2], has summarised the synthetic nature of facet systems: 'In facet classification no attempt is made to provide "ready-made" places for complex subjects. The scheme provides elementary terms from which the complex subjects are assembled'. This definition is very apt for the English Electric scheme, which abounds in devices for synthesising themes and more complex concepts from simple concepts. Recently much research has been done on the nature of these 'elementary terms'. The latest Cranfield project[3] made a distinction between a single term, a concept, and a theme. For example:

Theme
effect of stage characteristics on axial flow compressor stage performance

47

Concepts
axial flow compressor
stage performance
stage characteristics
Single terms
axial; flow; compressor; stage; performance; characteristics

While it is not difficult to recognise a theme and a single term, the nature of the concept is more difficult to define. A concept could be a single term—'flow' for example. It could contain two or three or more terms—such as 'hot forging' or 'colour television receivers' or 'transistor amplifiers'. Where the concept may be readily split into two or more simpler concepts—for example 'colour television systems' and 'receivers'; 'transistors' and 'amplifiers'—the concept is said to be at a 'high combination level' or 'highly precoordinated'.

In the light of this recent research it is now possible to look at the 'concepts' in the English Electric scheme third edition and to discern a generally low level of combination. Take for example:

Theme
'Wear tests on gears with solid lubricants for control rods in graphite moderated carbon dioxide cooled reactors'

Concepts

Average level	*English Electric level*
wear tests	*Lower level* wear (Plpp) and tests (Xt)
solid lubricants	*Lower level* lubricants (Lb) and solids (ahb)
gears	*Same level* Gears (Jm)
control rods	*Same level* control rods (Ff)
graphite moderated carbon dioxide reactors	*Lower level* graphite moderated reactors (Dkc) *and* carbon dioxide cooled reactors (Dkq) (combined class number Dkcq)

Class number   Dkcq Ff Jm Lb ahb Plpp Xt

From this example it can be seen that the English Electric scheme does not list the concept 'wear tests', for instance. This has to be built up by the classifier at the indexing stage. The example also illustrates the use of another synthetic device, the 'common attributes' schedule (see table 4A). This lists common properties such as size, shape and motive power. The attribute 'solid' is taken from this schedule to synthesize the concept 'solid lubricants'. Also illustrated is another synthetic device, occurring mainly in the machine section of the scheme, which enables the classifier to build up notation for devices classified by several attributes, without repeating the facet indicator (see tables 4B and 4C). In the example above the concept *graphite moderated carbon dioxide cooled reactor* (Dkcq) is synthesised from (see table 4B):

Dkc graphite moderated reactors

Dkq carbon dioxide cooled reactors

Similarly, *opposed piston V cylinder scavenged diesel engines* (Dedgm) is synthesised from (see table 4C):

Ded opposed piston engines

Deg v cylinder diesel engines

Dem scavenged diesel engines

B.2.1. *Low concept combination level*: *advantages and disadvantages*: During the operation of the scheme, the disadvantages of the low combination level of the concepts have become very apparent: *a*) There is a danger that the classifier will make up different class numbers for the same concept, so that like information is separated in the index. For example the term 'solid lubricant' could be made up either from 'lubricant' (Lb) combined with 'solid' (ahb) from the common attributes schedule to make Lb ahb; or by combining 'lubricant' (Lb) with Mahb, the notation for 'solids' in the materials facet, to form the class number Lb Mahb. *b*) The device for classifying machines by their attributes without repeating the facet indicator can complicate the catalogue and hamper recall. For example, if the user is searching for 'scavenged diesel engines' he cannot look only under Dem (scavenged diesel engines) but must search also under diesel engines classified primarily by other attributes, for example Degm, Dejm, Dedgm, and so on (see table 4C). *c*) Since well-used, familiar concepts have to be synthesised from simple concepts, they do not appear in the index to the schedules or in the body of the tables. There are two disadvantages in this. The first is that, since they do not feature in the schedules, they cannot be shown in relation to other terms with which they are associated. This is the case for 'television receivers', which does not occur as a concept in the third edition but must be synthesised from 'television' and 'receivers'. In a thesaurus or enumerative classification this concept would be listed, probably with appropriate circuits and components shown related to it. The second disadvantage is that casual users of the schedules are soon discouraged if they cannot find frequently sought terms in the index. This difficulty is overcome in the English Electric libraries where all the synthesised terms are included in the index to the catalogues.

The advantages of a low concept coordination level are as follows: *a*) The system does give a high degree of hospitality. Many new concepts can be accommodated without adding to the schedules, particularly using the common attributes tables. *b*) The schedules are brief and concise.

In the new edition it is likely that the combination level will be raised. The term ' television receivers ' will exist as a scheduled concept, for instance. Many concepts will still be synthesised from simpler concepts; but many of these will appear in the index and in the appropriate place in the tables, with instructions indicating to the classifier how the notation is to be built up. This will be the case for electron tube applications. For instance, under ' amplifiers ' the category ' electron tube amplifiers ' will appear, but with instructions to represent it with the notation for amplifiers, combined with the notation for electron tubes and all species of electron tubes. The common attributes schedules may be retained but their use may be restricted. As for the synthesising device for diesel engines and other machines, it is likely that this will be abandoned. Machines with several attributes will be classified according to each attribute separately. However, if a machine or device is commonly classified by more than one attribute—for example, a particular type of reactor—the type will be enumerated in the schedules and will occur in the index.

C THESAURUS/FACET INTERACTION

It has always been the practice when constructing a facet classification to examine first the terms and concepts in the field to be classified and, by analysing these, to discover appropriate categories and facets. During the revision of the English Electric scheme, and particularly in the revision of the electronics and communication engineering sections, the examination of terms and concepts is being done with the help of thesaurus techniques. For each concept a thesaurus form is completed (see table 5A). The thesaurus includes a definition of the concept. It also shows broader terms (BT), narrower terms (NT), and terms over which the concept is given preference (UF). These latter may be synonyms, near synonyms, narrower terms, or confounded word endings. Finally, the thesaurus lists terms related in a way other than hierarchically (RT). After the concepts for a particular subject area are recorded on the thesaurus forms, a classification schedule is devised based on the thesaurus concepts.

The concepts in the thesaurus and the concepts in the classification are the same concepts. By marrying the thesaurus and the classification scheme, it is hoped that the fourth edition will benefit from the interaction of facet and thesaurus construction techniques, as follows:

1 The thesaurus shows relationships which cannot easily be displayed in classification schedules. Facet schedules display only related terms within the facet—a thesaurus can also show cross-references to terms in different categories. 1a) Some concepts have more than one broader term or genus. This can be readily shown in a thesaurus, but not easily in a class schedule. For example, ' trigatrons ' could be classified as ' gas discharge tubes ' or as ' cold cathode tubes '. When a facet classification and thesaurus are combined, as they will be in the fourth edition of the English Electric scheme, this additional information about the term could appear in the thesaurus index or in the schedules—the term appearing with an asterisk under the heading which has not been preferred (see table 5B). 1b) The ' related terms ' (RT) in the thesaurus give additional information about the concept, much of which may not be expressed in a classification schedule. This is particularly the case where the concept is related to a term in another category or facet. A related term may show whole/part relationships: for example, electron tubes/anodes. It may show a process or property relationship: for example, vibration/vibration measurement, space vehicles/guidance, gas discharge tubes/gas discharges. It may show applications and effect: for example, x-rays/x-ray analysis, friction/lubrication, gamma rays/radiation effects. In the thesaurus-based fourth edition it is hoped that the additional information provided by the thesaurus will be retained, either as RT references in the thesaurus index or as cross-references introduced by asterisks in the tables (see table 5c). However, only a selective number of the related terms on the original thesaurus forms will be treated this way, partly for reasons of economy and partly because some of the related terms are too marginal to be valuable.

2 The thesaurus, in addition, provides another useful service. It tabulates under the preferred concept all synonyms, near synonyms and other terms referred to it. This type of information was not available in the third edition, but it will be in the fourth edition, where it is intended to make ' lead-in ' entries in the index from all subsumed terms to the preferred term. It is not yet decided whether to list

synonymous terms in the facet tables. In some cases this would not be feasible; for instance, where there are three or more synonyms for one term.

3 The thesaurus also provides better editorial control of word form. Rules are laid down concerning inverted or direct entries, plural and singular forms and punctuation, for example.

4 Should the thesaurus-based facet schedules be required for a mechanised system with single terms—bearing in mind the findings of the second Cranfield project[3], which showed the possible superiority of single terms in mechanised retrieval—the controlled and edited terms of the fourth edition could readily be reduced to single terms.

Although combining a thesaurus with facet schedules improves the schedules, the reciprocal effect is equally important. D J Campbell[4] found a facet classification valuable for a radical revision of an existing keyword list. He makes the point that facet analysis brings together all keywords related to a particular topic and ensures that they represent distinct concepts. Facet analysis certainly enforces greater precision in thesaurus construction. If a concept has to be put into a classification schedule a definite decision has to be made as to its relationship with other terms in that schedule—whereas without this discipline in thesaurus compilation there is a temptation to keep the relationship vague under the RT category.

D. METHODS OF CO-ORDINATION

D.I. *Postco-ordination:* The facet schedules are used by the English Electric libraries to classify manual catalogues and therefore must employ a preco-ordinate rather than a postco-ordinate method. In preco-ordination, the classifier combines the concepts to form class numbers at the indexing stage, in contrast to postco-ordination where the concepts are listed ' free ' at the indexing stage and combined only at the searching stage. There is no reason why the English Electric schedules should not be used postco-ordinately in a mechanised system. The facet notation or the word form of the concepts could be used as postco-ordinate descriptors. A test was in fact made to discover the potential of the English Electric scheme in postco-ordination during the WRU investigation[5] which showed that the recall of the permuted facet catalogue could be raised by postco-ordination by five percent with only three percent loss of precision.

D.2. *Preco-ordination: preferred order and chain index:* There are a number of ways in which concepts may be combined to form class numbers in facet and other classification systems: but when the English Electric system was devised the usual practice was to use facet classifications with the 'preferred order and chain index' co-ordination method, and so this system was adopted. This decision undoubtedly reduces the performance obtainable by the system; but in spite of this the English Electric libraries still retain the chain index. The case against the chain index has been well documented[6, 7, 8] and so it will be no more than briefly summarised here.

With preferred order and chain index, the concepts are arranged according to a predetermined order. In the English Electric scheme the order gives priority as follows: 'machines', 'components', 'materials', 'physical phenomena', 'operations', 'instruments'. In this way, the class number for the theme *fatigue of steam turbine steel alloy blades* is co-ordinated as follows in *the preferred order*

Machines	Components	Materials	Physical phenomena
steam turbines	blades	steel alloys	fatigue
(Db)	(Je)	(Ns.g)	(Pk)

The co-ordinated class number is Db Je Ns.g Pk.

Since only the first concept (Db) will appear in the catalogue in the filing position, some device must be used to locate the remaining concepts in the class number—the distributed facets. This device is the *chain index* which arranges the concepts in the reverse order to that of the co-ordinated class numbers, as follows:

FATIGUE: steel alloys: blades: steam turbines	Db Je Ns.g Pk
STEEL ALLOYS: blades: steam turbines	Db Je Ns.g
BLADES: steam turbines	Db Je
STEAM TURBINES	Db

These terms are, of course, arranged in alphabetical order in the chain index.

There are several disadvantages of the preferred order and chain index techniques. These are the scatter of facets in the class sequence and the one-directional and other limitations in the arrangement of concepts in the chain index.

D.2.1 *Scattered facets in the class sequence* (see table 6): Although the user may find in the chain index the whereabouts of the concepts he requires—that is, in which co-ordinated numbers they are located —the search is not then completed. The next stage involves checking through the class sequence to find these class numbers before the actual references may at last be consulted. It is unfortunate that in the English Electric libraries the preferred order chosen is not, in fact, the best for the heaviest users of the catalogue—the research and development engineers and scientists, who are usually concerned with a problem or process irrespective of its application to a particular machine or component. For them it is particularly frustrating that their subject interests are widely scattered under what appear to be marginal or irrelevant headings. Another difficulty which arises in the chain index is that the entries for a certain term (usually one from the problem or process facet) become so numerous that the user may be discouraged from checking the index and may never proceed to the classified catalogue. Six years ago there were over a hundred entries under the term ' fatigue ' in the chain index. Since then, the English Electric libraries have begun to make additional entries directly under ' fatigue ' in the classified catalogue and have treated similar problem concepts likewise. They have also tried to reduce ' scatter ' by limiting the number of terms allowed in combination and in making two or more parallel chains for a complex class number rather than one very long chain. In this way they have moved towards a measure of permutation in the catalogue.

D.2.2. *One-directional arrangement of the concepts in the chain index:*
It is obvious that the concepts in the chain index are associated in one direction only—that is, the reverse of the class number. For example, in the case of a class number ABCD, the chain index locates only concepts arranged in the reverse direction as follows:

DCBA	DCB	DC	D
CBA	CB	C	
BA	B		
A			

The chain index will not locate concepts arranged in the forward direction as follows:

AB+
AC+
AD+
BC+
BD+
CD+

The mechanised programme[9] for the print-out of the chain index partly overcomes the one-directional problem by repeating the complete chain after the print-out of each keyword, thus:

D	CBA
C	DCBA

B   DCBA

A   DCBA

D.2.3. *Intervening concepts in the chain index:* It is also possible to miss concepts in the chain index if the two concepts required occur together in the chain but are separated from each other by another concept (see again table 6). For example:

Sought concepts	Intervening concepts
CA	CBA
DB	DCB
DA	DCBA

This difficulty is less apparent when the index is printed out than when the searcher is scanning cards in a catalogue drawer.

D.3. *Co-ordination methods*: *permutation:* With permutation the constituent concepts of a class number are combined without preferred order. This involves making several class numbers with different arrangement of the concepts in each. Usually a class number is made for each constituent concept in the filing position; additional class numbers could also be made with the subsequent concepts permuted. In 'free' permutation there are no set rules and the selection of the permutations is done intuitively by those with a knowledge of the classification and the needs of the users. In this way, a class number with three concepts ABC could be arranged into six permuted class numbers (see table 7A):

ABC

ACB

BAC

BCA

CAB

CBA

but this would usually be reduced to three or four entries. To search a permuted catalogue the user checks the index for the class numbers of the concepts required. If there are three concepts he could try six searches with the three terms combined in different permutations. If this fails he could search again on combinations of the two terms. Lastly, if this also fails, he could search on each term singly. This type of search is on average quicker than one via the chain index. For instance, the user would have to search only three areas in the catalogue, that is A+, B+ and C+. The great danger, however, of permutation is that the number of entries per document in the class sequence might be greater than those in a chain index and preferred order catalogue, especially where a class number contains more than three concepts.

There are two methods of permutation which reduce the number of permutations to be made in an arbitrary manner. These are J R Sharp's SLIC principle[10] (see table 7B) and a system used with the *London education classification*[2] and elsewhere (see table 7C) which permutes by underlining each concept in turn and filing them by the underlined concept (the ' rotated index ' system).

It is possible that some form of permutation will be used with the fourth edition in manual catalogue applications. There has already been a precedent for the use of this method. The English Electric schedules were used with success with permutation in the WRU test[5]. Another factor in favour of permutation is that the facet system in the first Cranfield test[6] showed a five percent increase in recall when permutation was used.

E. PERFORMANCE TESTS

No conclusive assessment can be made of the efficiency of the English Electric classification without a performance test; but no recent investigation has been made, although a test was carried out as long ago as 1961 by the ASLIB Cranfield Project.[11] In this test the recall figure was 77·4 percent. According to these figures the English Electric scheme performed rather better than the facet classification tested in the first Cranfield project[6]. However, these figures may not be very meaningful, as the test was made before Cranfield had developed more precise techniques for measuring systems performance. The test was based on the recall of source documents only, and does not give a complete recall/precision figure. Earlier this year, however, the English Electric Central Library made a survey of users' reactions to the classification system[12] and it is interesting to note that twenty eight percent found it ' easy to understand ', twenty four percent ' not easy, but no great problem ' and only eight percent ' very difficult '.

F. CONCLUSION

Seven years' experience with the English Electric classification scheme seems to show that a facet scheme can operate as successfully as other schemes, although without precise results it is not possible to prove this claim. The third edition of the scheme has flaws in the basic structure, tends to have too low a level of concept combination, and its efficiency is reduced by the preferred-order method of co-ordination used. Nevertheless the scheme appears to be a fairly adequate indexing language and is accepted as such by those who have to operate it. It is intended that the fourth edition, with its thesaurus/facet structure, will not only bring the schedules up to date but will overcome many of the shortcomings of earlier editions. If this is achieved the English Electric faceted classification for engineering may have many years of useful life ahead as an indexing language for manual and machine systems. If this is true for the English Electric scheme, it may also be true for all facet schemes.

REFERENCES

1 Binns, J and Bagley, D: *A faceted subject classification for engineering.* Whetstone (Leics), English Electric Company Ltd third edition 1961.
2 Foskett, D J: *The London education classification.* London, University, Institute of Education, 1964 (*Education libraries bulletin,* supplement 6).
3 Cleverdon, C W and others: *Factors determining the performance of indexing systems.* Cranfield, College of Aeronautics, 1966.
4 Campbell, D J: *Application of classificatory methods to radical revision of thesauri or lists of keywords.* Oxford, Pressed Steel Company Ltd (private circulation).
5 Aitchison, Jean and Cleverdon, C W: *A report on a test of the index of metallurgical literature of the Western Reserve University.* Cranfield, College of Aeronautics, 1963
6 Cleverdon, C W: *Report on the first stage of an investigation into the comparative efficiency of indexing systems.* Cranfield, College of Aeronautics, 1960. *Report on the testing and analysis of an investigation into the comparative efficiency of indexing systems.* Cranfield, College of Aeronautics, 1962.
7 Aitchison, Jean: ' The English Electric classification ' *Journal of documentation,* 18 (2) June 1962, pp 80-88. (Classification Research Group Bulletin, no 8.)
8 Aitchison, Jean: ' Case history: the English Electric scheme ' (*in* Vickery, B C: *Faceted classification schemes.* New Brunswick (NJ), Rutgers University Press, 1966).
9 Dowell, N G and Marshall, J W: ' Experience with computer produced indexes ' ASLIB *Proceedings,* 14 (10) October 1962, pp 323-332.
10 Sharp, J R: ' The SLIC index ' (*in* ASLIB: *Looking forward in documentation: proceedings of the 38th annual conference, Exeter 1964.* London, ASLIB, 1964, pp 2-11 to 2-16.
11 Warburton, B and Cleverdon, C W: *Report on the first stage of a test on the library catalogue of the English Electric Co Ltd, Whetstone.* Cranfield, College of Aeronautics, 1961.
12 Ireland, R E: *Survey of Whetstone central library users.* Whetstone (Leics), English Electric Company Ltd, 1967 (W/ML p 10).

TABLE I

ANALYTICAL CHARACTERISTICS: *Examples taken from the English Electric Classification*

A *Organic coatings* (3rd edition)
- Le paints and enamel paints, organic coatings
- Lf varnishes, lacquers
- Lg enamels
     further division of Le/g

  By composition:
- b oil based
- c synthetic
- d synthetic oil treated

  By purpose:
- h external
- j internal
- k filler
- l primer
- m undercoating
- n thinner

  By pigment:
- r use Mw for division by chemical content

  By vehicle:
- s use Mw and My for division by chemical composition

  By method of hardening:
     use r/y only where it is necessary to emphasise these charac-
     teristics

- tb oxidation
- td polymerization
- tg air drying
- th stoving

  By solvent properties:
- vb water solvent

  By type of finish:
- yb matt
- yd semi-matt
- yg glossy

58

table 1 continued

B *Photography* (draft 4th edition)
    *photochemistry
    *photocopying
    *printing
    *xerography

     By type:
    flash photography
    colour photography
    infrared photography
    laser photography
    stereophotography
    high speed photography
    shadow photography
    schlieren photography
    microphotography
    aerial photography
    astronomical photography
    underwater photography

    Photographic processes
    *focusing
    *photochemistry
    exposure (photography)
    development (photography)
    enlargement (photography)

    Photographic equipment
    *optical filters
    *lenses
    *flash lamps
    cameras
    projectors

    Photographic materials
    photographic film
    photographic plates
    photographic paper
    photographic emulsion
    photographic fixatives

table 1 continued

c *Capacitors* (draft 4th edition)

By purpose:
*protective capacitors
fixed capacitors
   *electrolytic capacitors
   *paper capacitors
variable capacitors
   *varactors
   differential capacitors
   straight line capacitors
   trimmer capacitors
   vibrating capacitors
   synchronous capacitors
blocking capacitors
commutating capacitors
noninductive capacitors
guard-ring capacitors
guard-well capacitors

By materials or methods of construction:
*varactors
*synchronous capacitors
ceramic capacitors
electrolytic capacitors
paper capacitors
mica capacitors
pressure type capacitors
thin film capacitors

TABLE 2

ENGLISH ELECTRIC FACETED CLASSIFICATION FOR ENGINEERING: FUNDA-
MENTAL CATEGORIES AND PRIMARY FACETS IN THE THIRD EDITION

A *Fundamental categories*

    industries (personality)
    machines and systems (personality)
    ancillary plant and components (personality)
    materials (matter)
    physical phenomena (energy)
    operations (energy)
    agent (instruments and equipment) (personality)
    language and form divisions
    geographical divisions (space)

B *Primary facets*

A	industries
B/E	machines and systems
B	electrical systems and machines
C	telecommunication systems and plant
D	mechanical and thermal plant and machines
E	transport systems and machines
F/K	ancillary plant and components
F	special components
G	electric and electronic circuits
H	electric ancillary plant and components
I	electronic components
J	mechanical sub-assemblies and components
K	mechanical components
L/N	materials
L	materials according to use
M	materials according to composition: compound substances
N	materials according to composition: elements, metals, alloys
O/T	physical phenomena
O	chemical phenomena and properties
OA	astronomical, geological and meteorological phenomena
P	physics of solids
Q	fluid mechanics, heat, thermodynamics
R	electricity and magnetism
S	nuclear, atomic and molecular physics
T	theoretical physics, mechanics, sound, vibrations, light
U/Y	operations
U	specialised operations
V	production engineering
W	management
Y	mathematics
Z	agent (instruments and equipment)

TABLE 3

ENGLISH ELECTRIC FACETED CLASSIFICATION FOR ENGINEERING: MAIN
FACETS PROPOSED FOR THE FOURTH EDITION

SCIENCE
PHYSICS
ASTRONOMY, METEOROLOGY, GEOPHYSICS
CHEMISTRY
BIOLOGY, MEDICINE
METALLURGY
MATERIALS

TECHNOLOGY
ENGINEERING
RELATED TECHNOLOGY
RELATED TECHNIQUES

SOCIOLOGICAL ENVIRONMENT
Auxiliary schedules
Common attributes
Form division
Geographical divisions
Language divisions

TABLE 4

SYNTHETIC FEATURES: *Examples showing special synthetic devices occurring in the third edition of the English Electric Facet Classification*

A *Excerpt from common attributes schedules (3rd ed), p 155*

ac/g	Motive power
ag	thermal
agb	steam
agc	geothermal
agd	hot air, gas
agf	liquid fuel
agg	solid fuel
ags	solar
agy	multi-fuel, dual-fuel
ah	State
ahb	solid
ahc	mixtures, semi-solids
ahd	fluid
ahe	gas
ahec	compressed, liquid gas
ahf	liquid, molten
ahg	colloid, suspensions
ahh	emulsions
ahi	foams
ahj	aerosols
ahk	slurries
ahl	solutions
ahm	pulp
ahn	film
ahp	dispersion
ahv	2 phase
ahvc	3 phase
ahve	4 + phase
	to indicate solids, liquids, gases, etc generally use мah and divisions
ai	Manufactured form of materials
	see also al schedules for shape
aib	yarn
aic	woven, cloth, fabric
aid	braid, plait
aie	felt
aif	tape
aig	mesh, webbing, network
ail	laminated, board
aim	reinforced
aip	powder, flake, pulverised (use avı for powdered metal)

table 4 continued

B *Excerpt from nuclear reactors schedules (3rd ed)*
  ᴅkb/g thermal
    By moderator:

ᴅkc	graphite
ᴅkcb	beryllium
ᴅkd	water, light
ᴅkdb	boiling water
ᴅkdd	pressurised water
ᴅke	water, heavy
ᴅkeb	boiling water
ᴅked	pressurised water
ᴅkf	hydrogen, hydrides
ᴅkg	organic compounds

    By coolant:

m	gas
n	air
p	hydrogen
q	carbon dioxide
r	helium
rn	nitrogen and other gases
s	water, light
sb	boiling, steam
sd	pressurised
t	water, heavy
tb	boiling, steam
td	pressurised
u	organic
v	liquid metals
vb	bismuth
vl	lithium
vm	mercury
vp	potassium
vs	sodium

table 4 continued

c *Excerpt from diesel engine schedules (3rd ed)*
DE   diesel engines, compression ignition engines★

   By cycles:
DEC   two stroke
         use DE for 4-stroke

   By arrangement of pistons:
DED   opposed

   By arrangement of cylinders (if not in line):
DEG   v shape
DEH   delta
DEJ   special

   By charging system (if not naturally aspirated):
DEM   scavenged
DEP   pressure charged (for turbo, superchargers see DR)
DEQ   pressure charged, intercooled

   By fuel:
DES   dual fuel, multi fuel
DETM   natural gas burning
DETR   residual fuel

   By cooling system:
DEWE   evaporative water (phase change)
DEWF   fuel oil cooled

   By ignition/compression:
DEX   combined CI spark ignition engine (spark-CI)

         Further divide by application using auxiliary schedules etc,
         eg
         DE-R   diesel engines—for mines
         DE AEI diesel engines—for automobiles
         Use BPF for diesel powered electric power stations

TABLE 5

THESAURUS/FACET INTERACTION: *Examples taken from the English Electric Faceted classification, 4th edition (draft).*
A example of a thesaurus form

ENGLISH ELECTRIC CENTRAL LIBRARY
THESAURUS FORM

Term	Facet class number	Associated terms	Nature of relationship			
			UF	NT	BT	RT
ANODES						
Scope notes						
EJC						
Graf. Anode. The positive electrode such as the plate of a vacuum tube: the element to which the principal stream of electrons flows. 2. in a cathode-ray tube, the electrodes connected to a source of positive potential. These anodes are used to concentrate and accelerate the electron beam focusing		plates (anodes)	UF			
		inert anodes	UF			
		sacrificial anodes?	UF			
		electrodes			BT	
		electron tube components			BT	
Handel. Anode. The electrode via which current enters a device. It is the positive terminal of an electroplating cell, but the negative terminal of a battery. 2. Any electrode in a thermionic valve or tube which is operated at an appreciably positive potential.		electrodeposition				RT
		electroplating				RT
		cathode ray tubes				RT
		thermionic tubes				RT
		vacuum tubes				RT
		gas discharge tubes				RT
		electrochemical electrodes				RT
		electron tubes				RT
Plate (USA)		collectors (transistors)				RT

table 5 continued

B *Concepts with more than one broader term* (BT).
Example taken from the draft schedule for electron tubes

ELECTRON TUBES

By construction:
Vacuum tubes
Note: use only for vacuum tubes generally.
*Details of all tubes in the category (but classified primarily in another category) could be listed here but they are numerous—and the details are available in the thesaurus.

Thermionic tubes
Note: use only for thermionic tubes generally.
*As for vacuum tubes.

Gas discharge tubes
*cold cathode glow discharge tubes
*neon tubes
*controlled cold cathode glow discharge tubes
*counting tubes
*detratrons
*trigatrons
*indicator tubes
ionization tubes
hot cathode arc discharge tubes
thyratrons
pool tubes
excitrons
ignitrons
plasma tubes
flash tubes
transmit-receive tubes (duplexes)

Cold cathode tubes
*counting tubes
*dekatrons
*phototubes
*photomultipliers
cold cathode glow discharge tubes
neon tubes
controlled cathode glow discharge tubes
indicator tubes (numerical)
trigatrons

67

3*

table 5 continued

> > *Electron wave tubes*
> > > travelling wave tubes
> > > > backward wave tubes
> > > > > carcinotrons
> > > > magnetrons

c *Concepts with related terms in other schedules* (RT)
Example taken from draft schedule for electricity

ELECTRICITY
   *wave properties and phenomena
   *electrical variables control
   *electrical measurements
   *electrochemistry
   *electrical faults

Electrodynamics
Current (electric)
*fault currents
*leakage currents
*short circuit currents
*impulse currents
*overcurrents
*current collection
*current control
*current measurement

   By type:
   alternating current
   direct current
   heavy current
   light current
   eddy current

   By phenomena:
   electrokinectics
   current distribution
   skin effect
   current reversal, commutation
   current collection
   rectification

Electric discharges
   *fault currents
   *leakage currents
   *short circuit currents

68

table 5 continued

breakdown (electric)
flashover
sparks

surface discharges
   corona
gas discharges
 *ionization
 *corona
 *breakdown (electric)
 *gas discharge tubes
 *sparks

TABLE 6

METHODS OF CO-ORDINATION: PREFERRED ORDER AND CHAIN INDEX

Disadvantages of preferred order and chain index

Distributed facets: example taken from the chain index at the English Electric Central Library (1961) (excerpt only)

FATIGUE	Pk
FATIGUE: aircraft structures	Eb Fc Pk
FATIGUE: aluminium	Nal Pk
FATIGUE: aluminium: plates	Kwe Nal Pk
FATIGUE: aluminium alloys	Nal.d Pk
FATIGUE: aluminium alloys: aircraft	Eb Nal.d Pk
FATIGUE: aluminium alloys: butt welds	Kywzb Nal.d Pk
FATIGUE: aluminium brass: tubes: inter-coolers: gas turbines	Dh Dx Kkh Nalcumn Pk
FATIGUE: aluminium magnesium alloys	Nalmg Pk
FATIGUE: arc welds: gun cones: aircraft	Eb Fsb Kywc Pk
FATIGUE: argon arc welds: gun cones: aircraft	Eb Fsb Kywd Pk
FATIGUE: austenitic stainless steel	Ns.l Pk
FATIGUE: ball bearings: bibliographies	21 Jtt Pk
FATIGUE: beams	Kwb Pk
FATIGUE: bearings	Jt Pk
FATIGUE: bellows	Kybm Pk
FATIGUE: bellows: gas circuits: CO_2 graphite reactors	Dkcq Fde Kybm Pk
FATIGUE: grey iron	Nfecp Pk
FATIGUE: heat resistant alloys: bibliographies	21 N.gt Pk
FATIGUE: helical compression springs	Kehs Pk
FATIGUE: high strength steel	Ns.hp Pk
FATIGUE: high tensile low alloy steel	Ns.hp Pk
FATIGUE: hoses	Kkp Pk
FATIGUE: hoses: grabheads: fuelling machines: CO_2 graphite reactors	Dkcq Fgc Klk Kkp Pk
FATIGUE: inconel	Nni cr Pk
FATIGUE: lead alloys: bearings: crankshafts: diesel engines	De Jbt Jt Npb.d Pk
FATIGUE: leaded steels	Ns.g Pb Pk
FATIGUE: light alloys	N.ec Pk
FATIGUE: light metals: bibliographies	21 N.ec Pk
FATIGUE: low alloy steels	Ns.h Pk
FATIGUE: low alloy steel: electroslag welds	Kywx Ns.h Pk
FATIGUE: low alloy steel: welds	Kyw Ns.h Pk
FATIGUE: magnesium alloys: cans: fuel elements: CO_2 graphite reactors	Dkcq Jg Kcm Nmg.d Pk

table 6 continued

FATIGUE: manganese nickel low alloy steel: blades: steam turbines	Db Je Ns.h Mn Ni Pk
FATIGUE: martensitic stainless steel: blades: steam turbines	Db Je Ns.m Pk
FATIGUE: metals	Pk
FATIGUE: metals: aircraft	Eb Pk
FATIGUE: mild steel	Ns.d Pk
FATIGUE: mild steel: pipes	Kkh Ns.d Pk
FATIGUE: mild steel: welds	Kyw Ns.d Pk
FATIGUE: mild steel: welds: pipes	Kkh Kyw Ns.d Pk
FATIGUE: mild steel plates: structures	Kwe Ns.d Pk
FATIGUE: mild steel welds: shafts	Jb Myw Ns.d Pk
FATIGUE: molybdenum low alloy steel: steam pipes	Kkh agb Ns.hKc Pk
FATIGUE: nickel	Nni Pk
FATIGUE: nickel chromium molybdenum low alloy steel: bolts: aircraft	Eb Kzk Ns.hNicrMo Pk
FATIGUE: nimonic alloys	Nni cr Pk
FATIGUE: nitrided steel	Ns avmpn Pk
FATIGUE: nuts	Kzn Pk
FATIGUE: plain bearings	Jtb Pk
FATIGUE: steel structures	Kv/w Ns Pk
FATIGUE: steels: bibliographies	21 Ns Pk
FATIGUE: structural steel	Kv/w Ns Pk
FATIGUE: structures, aircraft	Eb Fc Pk
FATIGUE: studs	Ksp Pk
FATIGUE: support pillars: traction DC motors	Bb aEk Kbs Pk
FATIGUE: surfaces	Kxsd Pk
FATIGUE: titanium alloys: bolts: aircraft	Eb Kzk Nti.d Pk
FATIGUE: tubes: hydraulic systems	Dd Kkh Pk
FATIGUE: uranium	Nu Pk
FATIGUE: valve springs: IC engines: bibliographies	21 De/i Jf Kd Ke Pk
FATIGUE: weld metals	Kyy Pk
FATIGUE: weld metals: high temperature steel welds	Kyw Ns.t Kyy Pk
FATIGUE: welded steel structures	Kv Kyw Ns Pk
FATIGUE: welded structures	Kv Kyw Pk
FATIGUE: welds	Kyw Pk
FATIGUE: welds: aircraft structures	Eb Fc Kyw Pk
FATIGUE: welds: structures	Kv Kyw Pk
FATIGUE: wire for springs	Ke Krt Pk
FATIGUE: wire ropes: bibliographies	21 Krs Pk

TABLE 7

A *'Free' permutation*: for example concepts ABC could produce six class numbers

ABC	
ACB	which may be reduced to three or four at
BAC	the discretion of the indexer—depending on
BCA	knowledge of the subject and the needs of
CAB	the users
CBA	

P SLIC *index*: A method put forward by J R Sharp to limit permuted entries. In this index terms (in word form) are combined in alphabetical order allowing the following combination only:

I	ABCD
2	ABD
3	ACD
4	AD
5	BCD
6	BD
7	CD
8	D

The number of combinations per number of terms co-ordinated is reduced by the SLIC index as follows:

No of terms assigned to the document	Full Permutation	Selected Combinations
2	2	2
3	6	4
4	24	8
5	120	16
6	720	32
7	5,000	64
8	40,320	128
9	362,880	256
IO	3,628,800	512

C *Permutation by underlining*

Class number ABC. Three entries A̲BC   AB̲C   ABC̲
Filing order of class numbers by underlining term:

A̲BC
AB̲C
ABC̲

This virtually gives only three entries—ABC BC C—as the filing is in one direction only, since the concepts on the left-hand-side of the underlined concepts are ignored in the arrangement of the cards in the catalogue.

CO-ORDINATE INDEXING

a practical approach

A JOHNSON
Technical librarian, British Insulated Callenders Cables Ltd, Prescot

IT IS JUST OVER eight years since I gave my first paper on co-ordinate indexing at an ASLIB Northern Branch conference only a few hundred yards from our present venue[1]. At that meeting the chairman, after the usual introductory remarks concluded by saying: ' having mastered the intricacies of the UDC Mr Johnson then turned his attention to other methods of information handling '. This rather startling and certainly exaggerated statement took me completely by surprise, but nevertheless provided an excellent introduction, since it was *because* I was not able to envisage myself as ever being the master of UDC that I endeavoured to find a system that offered some prospect of my being the master rather than the servant. I was in fact resentful of having to adapt myself to the system instead of bending the system to my own particular needs.

In saying this, I would not wish to give the impression that I had not a profound regard for the UDC and many other classification schemes that existed at that time and indeed still do, but for my particular application they did not provide the answer. The pre-determination of classes and sub-classes required an impossible prediction of subject matter yet to be documented and, more important still, of interests yet to be expressed. In common with many others, I had tried to expand certain sections of the UDC to meet my requirements. I had also tried surgery—the grafting-on of a well known metallurgical classification where it showed promise of being more effective for my needs, but all to no avail. I came to the conclusion that whereas classification was an excellent means of ordering the shelving of books in fairly wide classes, it was inadequate for the highly specialised literature with which we were dealing. The pace at which new scientific and technological developments were being made, and the corresponding influx of literature demanded a new approach to the handling of information. More than forty years after Fleming brought out his diode valve, based on Edison's earlier discovery of the principle of thermionic emission, we were still using valves operating on that same principle. Between 1948 and 1950 however, the work of people such as Bardeen, Brattain and Shockley resulted in the birth of the transistor. This was soon followed by molecular electronics and other solid-state devices, whereby it is now possible to build a whole amplifier on a sixpence. The point I am trying to make is that whereas in the past one had time to arrange and rearrange classification schedules, the present speed of scientific innovation is such that the process of addition or revision is far too slow and the prediction of new developments too

3**

difficult. The scientist, the engineer and the technologist are not only out-pacing the documentationalist, they are lapping him! New and faster methods of information handling were obviously needed and it is my opinion that co-ordinate indexing has provided for that need.

Since this talk is to be a practical approach I intend to concentrate on the problem as it affected my own Library at BICC, whom I hope you will all recognise as electric cable makers with a fairly wide variety of other interests such as copper refining, railway electrification, and, with their subsidiaries, builders of power and television masts, etc.

By far the greatest challenge was presented by the existence of a fairly large collection of internal research and technical reports covering a wide variety of subjects. It was quite inadequate to attempt to classify each report; indeed it was well nigh impossible, since their information content was too varied and too complex for any classification we could devise. Each report was not just one piece of information; it might contain dozens of pieces each of which might, at some time in the future be needed . . . not necessarily in the context of the main subject of the report. An attempt had in fact been made to classify these reports by a colleague from one of the Netherlands schools of documentation, but it failed on two main counts: the time taken to classify each report and the inability of anyone, other than the classifier, to effect retrieval.

We had not, at that time, the benefit of other people's experience of co-ordinate indexing apart from the 'Uniterm' system developed by Mortimer Taube, and already we had decided that our requirements demanded something more sophisticated. We had, in fact, used co-ordinate indexing some time before when it was applied to the indexing of correspondence. This was mainly administrative material, but the logical corollary was to apply the principle to other, more technical material. We express thoughts in words; concepts are even more meaningful, so why lose their sense in translating them into classification numbers? An elementary form of co-ordination with which most people are familiar can be found in books and articles of the 'materials selector' type. In this, one of the ordinates may be a list of metals, whilst the other may be a list of environments in which they may be expected to operate. The co-ordination of metal and environment reveals, in some cases, a symbol denoting compatibility or otherwise. Instead of a symbol, one might find a number representing a literature reference dealing with that particular combination. The limitations of this system will be obvious, the most obvious being the fact that it is limited in terms or concepts to any two and no more. Its inherent simplicity is, however, undisputed.

At this juncture it is difficult for me to avoid reiterating much that I said in my earlier paper on co-ordinate indexing and I hope I will be excused for so doing.

The first, and most vital step in the setting-up of a co-ordinate index is without doubt the painstaking process of constructing a thesaurus or dictionary of concepts. The thought and effort applied to this will eventually decide the efficiency of the system. I described how we set about this in my earlier paper and will not therefore repeat it. I am pleased to say that the forecast I then made of the total number of concepts we expected to use, was very substantially correct. The pre-co-ordination of terms to form meaningful concepts is, in our experience, well justified, since it imparts greater ' sense ' to the thesaurus and certainly eliminates many possible false sorts, or ' noise ', as some like to call them. A degree of classification or generic structuring can also be introduced to the thesaurus. For instance, we regard such phenomena as CORROSION, CRACKING, PITTING, FUNGAL ATTACK etc, as mechanisms of DETERIORATION and include them in the system under that heading. We group the ferrous metals such as iron and steel under the heading METALS and ALLOYS—ferrous, while aluminium, copper, tin etc are found under the generic METALS AND ALLOYS—non-ferrous. All items punched on the card for COPPER are also punched on the card for METALS AND ALLOYS—non-ferrous. By this means it is possible, by co-ordination of the cards DETERIORATION and COPPER, to determine what information exists on all forms of deterioration of copper; or alternatively, if one particular form of deterioration is required, say ' cracking ', this can readily be obtained by use of the cards for COPPER and CRACKING. We call this process of going from the specific to the generic ' posting-up ', but whether the term is used elsewhere I do not know. The practice is repeated in many parts of the thesaurus, those coming readily to mind being PLASTICS where individual materials are subordinated to the generic and CABLES—power, where every cable used to carry power, as opposed to signals or data, is included.

A section of the index is devoted to trade names, companies and, in the case of our own reports, to authors' names. If the properties of a material known by its trade name are required, the trade name can be selected from the appropriate section and the properties sought from the thesaurus. The author section permits quick access to the question ' what has so-and-so written on a specified subject?' The companies section enables us to keep track on discussions our engineers may have had with the companies concerned on any given subject.

Many people have asked me about false sorts, or the throwing up of information not pertinent to the search. Our experience has been that they are exaggerated in importance and to a large extent avoidable. I will be saying more about them later when discussing the use of links and roles. We discovered, right from the start of our index, that one effective way of preventing false sorts was the repetition in the index of words which can be used both as nouns and as adjectives. Examples are ' AIR ' and ' WATER '. We have two cards in the system for each and convey the adjectival use by simply adding a hyphen after the term. AIR, without the hyphen, implies its use as a noun, and consequently all information on air itself is recorded on this card while information on AIR PUMPS or AIR COMPRESSORS would be obtained by the co-ordination of the terms AIR- and PUMPS, or AIR- and COMPRESSORS.

I have, in the example quoted, intentionally introduced a possible pit-fall. It lies in the terms PUMPS and COMPRESSORS. In practice, much thought would be given to the existence in the thesaurus of both terms. A compressor is usually a pump. There may be—there are—several types of compressor . . . rotary, reciprocating and diaphragm for instance. All can be used as compressors, but they are pumps too? Are we dealing with synonymous terms? This is an example of how some information can be overlooked during a search. If it is decided that all compressors are in fact pumps then one term must be dropped. At least, the card for the term must be excluded from the system, but not the entry in the dictionary. In this, the entry would appear as ' COMPRESSORS see PUMPS '. An alternative treatment would be to include both terms as cards, and when dealing with pumps used specifically as compressors to punch both cards. In such cases the card for PUMPS is endorsed ' punch also COMPRESSORS where applicable '.

I could occupy considerable time on the construction of the thesaurus of terms and their arrangement. I have remarked on a previous occasion that, unlike in a hierarchical classification, there are no signposts to act as guides. The constructor must build by logical anticipation of his or her needs, giving emphasis to detail where it is needed and structuring where it offers advantage. Another feature of our own thesaurus is a section under the heading 'Adjectives—form or degree '. Within this section one finds such terms as LOW, HIGH,

FLAT, THIN, HOT, COLD, ROD, BAR, STRIP, etc. It is surprising how often they are used and how useful they can be. As BICC Ltd. are manufacturers of copper in many forms, the card for COPPER is riddled with holes, but when a question involving 'hot-rolled high-conductivity copper strip' occurs, the appropriate cards for HIGH, HOT and STRIP reduce enormously the number of items to be scanned.

The depth to which it is possible to index is governed by the number of concepts in the thesaurus—the greater the number, the greater the permissible depth, and the greater the specificity of re-called items. Fewer concepts will produce a larger number of documents but not all may turn out to be pertinent and they will need scanning to decide this point. I would emphasise one important point, however—that the coarser search will reveal all the information that exists. Properly organised, co-ordinate indexes may, on occasion, provide as false sorts information that is not pertinent, but they do reveal information if it is there. In other words, at the co-ordination stage it may appear that information exists when in fact it does not but if it does exist it will be revealed.

At BICC we have found it convenient to have separate sets of cards, or separate indexes, for different material, that is different types of literature, governed by two distinct thesauri. The sets are divided into a) *Technical and research reports*, b) *Published literature* from periodicals, c) *Miscellaneous publications* (pamphlets etc) and d) *Books*.

The technical reports index is the most detailed and is controlled by approximately 3,000 concepts. Indexing in depth is justified with this material, since it contains the results of expensive research and includes information not to be found elsewhere.

The index of published literature consists in the main, of articles which have been abstracted in our *Monthly information bulletin*. Terms in this section number approximately 1,600.

Miscellaneous publications are filed in numeric sequence by accession number in transfer cases, which makes their recall by the index quick and convenient. The terms used are similar in scope and number to those used in b) above.

The mention of books and co-ordinate indexing can always be relied upon to stimulate interest and we are, as far as I know, the only library using co-ordinate indexing in this field of application.[2] We did not adopt it from choice but of necessity. Our shelving space was severely limited and it became obvious that leaving space for the extension of classes would soon be impossible. We therefore filled the shelves to capacity using the accession number of each book as its retrieval number. Naturally this produced a confusing mixture of unrelated subjects and considerable work in analysing each book and posting its information content to appropriate cards. Reference works such as the standard handbooks on various engineering sciences were not included, nor were encyclopedias, dictionaries and the like. Since most of the latter are ' reference only ' items, it was both convenient and fortuitous that they should be shelved separately.

Since most of our enquiries are for information rather than for specific books, the users of the library were not unduly perturbed, although the expression on the faces of newcomers is quite entertaining. I must make it clear that I do not recommend the system, although it has its advantages which I will outline later, but if we could revert to a position offering unlimited shelf-space I would return to a classified arrangement. Nevertheless I think I would still maintain a unit-concept index, but instead of retrieval being directly from the shelf it would be via the accession card. Such an arrangement would be more conventional and would satisfy everybody. I mentioned the advantages . . . the finding of information is certainly facilitated, particularly if it lies in a book the title of which does not suggest its presence there. In many libraries the memory and experience of the librarian is often called upon here, but the unit-concept index dispenses with this and enables the less experienced to provide the right book to answer a query. Marginal advantages lie in the fact that the latest additions are congregated together, while shelving errors are reduced to a very minimum—a first-day junior can do it. The dictionary of terms, which is distinct from the actual cards in the system, incorporates a considerable number of ' see ' references to enable non-technical staff to provide a book on a technical subject. A standard author catalogue is maintained.

A further unique feature arose when we started to index books, as it became obvious that some kind of ' weighting device ' was necessary when selecting material via the index. For example, assume an enquiry for a book giving information on ' bridges ' in the electrical sense. Bridges are used in electrical measurements, and a chapter on them will be found in almost any book on electrical engineering in general, and certainly in any book on electrical measurements. Thus, if one came across a chapter on bridges in a book on measurements in general, it would be recorded by punching the card for BRIDGES—

(elec). Suppose now the classic reference *Bridge methods* by Hague comes up for indexing; the same card must be punched in exactly the same way, but there is no comparison between the information content of the first book and that of Hague—the one a chapter, the other a monograph. We decided that this would not do and designed a second card-punch which incorporated a triangular die to punch a triangular hole in the card. This enabled us to differentiate between such books. The first book would be recorded by means of a round hole, whilst the second would be indicated by a triangular hole. The instruction to staff is therefore to ' read-off ' triangular entries first when selecting references. The triangle has a further use for denoting emphasis. In a book entitled *Electricity in mining,* for instance, the emphasis is upon the electrical aspect and very little real information is contained on mining. The punching for the electrical aspect is therefore done with the triangular punch, whilst that for the mining aspect is done with the circular punch. It should be noted that co-ordination is still achieved, as it is still possible to detect the light through the card, but the reader is at once aware where the emphasis lies. Members of the audience will no doubt have realised that this type of dual punching can be used in other ways also.

One cannot speak of a practical approach without an early consideration of cost, be it in terms of initial outlay, running cost or hidden costs in terms of time. On each of these factors co-ordinate indexing can compete with any other system. The many visitors we have had to our library have provided evidence that cost is a very important factor, particularly when selling the idea to their managements. With this in mind, my colleague Mr K J Baker prepared a paper on the economics of co-ordinate indexing, which he read at the ASLIB Northern Branch conference in 1966 at Llandudno[3]. In this paper Mr Baker includes a considerable amount of information on indexing and punching times, the cost and capacity of hardware and softwear, or ' tubs ' (as the card receptacles are called), and cards. Some of the punching times are incredibly small, but I can vouch for their authenticity since they were derived from our own library. In addition, Mr Baker has produced a simple sketch of a wooden box for accommodating about 1,500 × 4,000 module cards which can be constructed quite easily and cheaply for the benefit of those who wish to conduct a ' trial run ' before embarking on a full-scale venture.

One of the most controversial topics in co-ordinate indexing lies in the use or otherwise of links and roles. When we set up our index about ten years ago, links and roles had not been invented, or at least the terminology had not. A link may be defined as a device capable of showing that two or more terms used to index a document are related to each other within the context of that document. Roles are defined as codes for synthetic relationships used to modify the meaning of major descriptors. Both are intended to increase the efficiency of the search and to eliminate 'noise'. Although we were not conscious of the terms, we recognised the need for such devices and as a result we endeavoured to meet it by pre-co-ordination in those areas where 'noise' might be anticipated, and by the use of generic structuring. Another example of 'noise' avoidance is in our repetition of some terms as, for example, TWISTING. This can be a fault or a process; the term is therefore included twice: TWISTING (process) and TWISTING (fault). In effect this is a role indicator. Whether links and roles are necessary in any particular index is purely a matter for the indexer to decide, and this decision will be tempered by the recall efficiency. I am ready to admit that in some fields, such as chemical processing, they may be very necessary. Another factor to be considered is the inflation of the vocabulary by their use, and here serious thought must be given before introducing them, although if the index is computerised the problem is not so acute. A very succinct summary on the use of links and roles has been provided by Mortimer Taube[4], while, more recently, papers by Jones[5] and Blagden[6] are worthy of mention.

I now intend to make a few comments on some of the very practical issues involved in co-ordinate indexing. Firstly, cards. We have found that most people set out to use the highest capacity card they can find when setting up their index. This is not always a good thing. On large capacity cards the squares into which holes are to be punched are very small, and as a result punching is, of necessity, precise. One has therefore to consider the person actually carrying out the punching and realise that the smaller the hole the greater the concentration required and the greater the fatigue involved. As most people start off with a large back-log of material to be indexed, fatigue is important because it affects output. Again, the larger type of card usually requires the operator to use *both* hands to extract and replace it in the file, and ergonomically this is bad. I will not go into detail on this point but I can assure you that if a person does nothing but punching all day long he will discover what I mean.

Still on the subject of cards, we have found many who are attracted to the more sophisticated type of punch, in which the ordinates are set up by means of graduated scales and an electrically operated drill permits the drilling of several holes at a time. This is not necessarily the fastest method, and furthermore it demands card-stock of high dimensional stability (especially when using large cards with small holes) and very accurate printing. It can in fact almost double the cost of cards. One should also bear in mind the fact that once a set of cards has reached its capacity, it is not economic to leave them in the tubs they occupied while being punched. Thus some provision must be made for their filing in less expensive equipment. This dictates that the size of the card should be such that it can be filed in a standard size filing cabinet and not require a ' special '. Our own 4,000 module card was designed with these factors in mind and can be filed in a standard quarto filing cabinet when it leaves the tub.

Card readers of the illuminated type have their uses, but demand that the numbers are either memorised or written down before retrieval of the documents. In our own library we prefer to take the cards with us to the source of the material and work through the co-ordinations until we find the information we are seeking. In some libraries, a flying-spot scanning device with a paper tape read-out may hold some advantage.

I know that many of you will be wondering when I am going to say something about computers. I have left mention of them to the last because I have concentrated on practical issues, and although computers do lend themselves to co-ordinate indexing, I feel that there are not many small special libraries where the undoubted efficiency of computerised retrieval is either necessary or can be justified on economic grounds. There is, as you will know, a drive towards centralised information storage and retrieval, and this is a commendable objective, although I cannot envisage the existence of any centralised information bureau which can take the place of highly specialised information units operating in very specific fields. It is in these areas that the small co-ordinate index will continue to serve its masters with characteristic efficiency.

REFERENCES

[1] Johnson, A: ' Experience in the use of unit concept co-ordinate indexing applied to technical reports ' *Journal of documentation*, 19 (3), September 1959, pp 146-55.
[2] Johnson, A: ' Practical applications of ' feature card ' systems: III ' ASLIB *Proceedings*, 15 (6), June 1963, pp 186-8.

[3] Baker, K J: ' Unit concept co-ordinate indexing: the cost of setting up and operating a system ' *Northern Aslib bulletin,* 11 (4), October/December 1966, pp 3-27.

[4] Taube, M: ' Notes on the use of roles and links in co-ordinate indexing ' *American documentation,* 12 (2), April 1961, pp 98-100.

[5] Jones, K P: ' The use of roles and links on a pre-co-ordination basis in optical coincidence systems ' ASLIB *Proceedings,* 19 (6), June 1967, pp. 195-9.

[6] Blagden, J F: ' How much noise in a role-free and link-free co-ordinate indexing system?' *Journal of documentation* 22 (3), September 1966, pp 203-9.

NATURAL LANGUAGE INDEXING
FOR AUTOMATED INFORMATION SYSTEMS

S T HIGHCOCK BA
Information Scientist, Unilever Research Laboratory, Port Sunlight, Wirral, Cheshire

AN IMPORTANT DEVELOPMENT in the field of information processing in recent years is the trend away from systems using co-ordinate and classified indexes as the basis for information storage and retrieval, towards automated computer-based systems using natural language. The most advanced of these systems are based on automatic text analysis and creation of data files, and are often on-line systems involving a dialogue between man and machine as part of their search procedure. These are still at an experimental stage. Less advanced systems involve human selection of natural terms from titles and texts and often the source for retrieval of documents indexed in this way is a computer produced permutation index (keyword-in-context index). I shall discuss mainly the problems encountered in indexing for and searching systems of this type.

Before this I would like to describe briefly some of the disadvantages of classified indexes.

SOME DRAWBACKS OF CLASSIFIED INDEXES

In indexing based on various forms of classification there are two intellectual processes which with experienced indexers are simultaneous rather than separate: evaluation of the contents of a document and adaptation of the essential parts of these to the conceptual framework of the classification. To do this effectively the indexer must have the skill and knowledge to be able to recognise the subject matter, to understand what the document is about. The indexer also faces the problem of the difficulty of interpreting the classification concepts consistently. It becomes important to impose some discipline on indexers to ensure consistency of definition with respect to time and change of indexers. Each time an indexing problem is encountered a precedent is set, and these precedents have to be recorded in some form of list of indexing conventions. So the indexing problem becomes further complicated by consultation of indexing aids and discussion of precedents with other indexers.

Another drawback to classified indexing is that specific contexts are lost by their reduction from natural language to the more general language of a classification. For example, using a classification developed at Unilever Research Laboratory, Port Sunlight, the trade name 'DOBS—055' would be reduced to 'dodecylbenzene', 'sulphonate' and 'Shell', indistinguishable from any similar Shell compounds.

In spite of the discipline imposed on indexers, difficulties sometimes occur when searching, using classified indexes. At Port Sunlight the classification mentioned above has about 800 concepts and can be used to index documents in some detail; but because of our difficulty in interpreting some of these concepts (or of conventions which have arisen from them) we often have to search widely, looking for several terms when one might have been adequate.

Drawbacks like these are leading to the adoption of information systems based on the most explicit available indexing language: natural language.

NATURAL LANGUAGE INDEXING

Before I discuss some of the problems associated with natural language indexing, I shall mention the output forms which are available for systems indexed in this way. Output can consist of printed indexes of the KWIC type, or data files stored on magnetic tape or disc where, for example, co-ordinate searches can be made for natural language descriptors. I shall discuss output later, mainly restricting myself to the subject of printed indexes.

In natural language indexing, the skill of the indexer is involved only once, in the selection of natural language terms (now referred to as descriptors). All that remains is for these selected descriptors and any other necessary data (titles, authors etc) to be converted into machine-readable form, and a computer can process the input data, producing indexes and data files of the type already mentioned.

In selecting descriptors from a document it is necessary to establish what sort of assessment the indexer should make of the contents of the document, or what viewpoint to adopt as a basis for this assessment. Should he try to establish the document's main theme and choose only keywords appropriate to this: or should he try and interpret the document from as many points of view as possible?

As an example of how the indexer's point of view (or background) affects his selection of descriptors, here is an abstract of a report indexed during an experiment on word-choosing carried out at Port Sunlight[1]. The abstract has been indexed by three people with contrasting backgrounds: a non-technical clerk, the author of the report, and an information scientist.

Assessment of the odour and colour of toilet soaps.
Rectangular lattice.
An assessment of the colour and odour of toilet soaps has been carried

out using a 4×5 rectangular lattice. In a $N \times M$ lattice, each member of the N group is compared with each member of the M group, *ie* $N \times M$ comparisons, whereas a round robin would require $\frac{1}{2}(N + M(N + M - 1))$ comparisons.

Keywords chosen by non-technical clerk	odour
	colour
	toilet
	soaps
Keywords chosen by author of report	colour
	odour
	rectangular
	lattice
Keywords chosen by information scientist	odour
	colour
	toilet
	soaps
	rectangular
	lattice

The words chosen by the non-technical clerk reflect her knowledge of some aspects of soap technology but she has missed entirely the statistical content of the abstract. The author's selection shows that he is really only interested in the statistical assessment of colour and odour: soap is a subsidiary subject. The information scientist by the nature of his occupation has a broader viewpoint than the other two and the words he has chosen reflect this: however he might have chosen ' assessment ' as well, a useful generic term which might help in eventual retrieval of the report.

The interesting fact emerges here that an unskilled indexer, the clerk, has managed to select a significant number of meaningful descriptors from the document: in other words, unlike classified indexing, an indexer selecting natural language descriptors needs only to recognise the subject matter of the report and not to understand it fully. However, the information scientist, trained to take as broad a view as possible of the contents of the document, is able to see the subject matter more clearly than the author or the clerk. The really significant thing about this indexing process, though, is that the main restraint found in co-ordinate indexing imposed by the conceptual framework of the index is not found here.

One danger in taking a broad view of a document's contents is that overindexing or multi-indexing may occur, especially if the full text of a document is scanned for indexing purposes. For example, 'dish-washing machine' may be selected as a descriptor in one part of the document and in another part of the report 'machine' might be selected from a phrase like—'dishes washed in the machine'. Multi-indexing does not matter so much when computer 'co-ordinate searching' is used, but it is unsuitable for printed indexes where every keyword provides an entry point to the index.

Another problem the indexer faces in the selection of keywords is the one of vocabulary control. This can mean the use of preferred grammatical forms, for example the choice of 'foam' in favour of 'foaming', 'foamed' as the noun from which the other forms are derived. Or the removal of special symbols from compound terms, for example 'oil water interface' instead of 'oil-water interface' or 'oil/water interface'. The ultimate step in vocabulary control is to adopt a list of keywords in their preferred forms, or better still an information retrieval or indexing thesaurus which lists the terms of the system vocabulary and exhibits relationships among these terms. An example of such a thesaurus is the *Thesaurus of engineering terms*[2]. Thesauri of this type which are used for indexing often have relationships of the type 'post on' or 'seen from' to indicate pre-ferred synonyms, as well as showing terms in a standardised spelling. I want to return to the use of thesauri and similar aids to indexing and enquiry-framing later, but for the moment I shall limit myself to saying that the use of various forms of vocabulary control at the indexing stage can soon lead to restraints on the indexer almost as severe as those obtaining in indexing using a classification.

SOME PROBLEMS OF INDEXING FOR KWIC AND SIMILAR PERMUTATION INDEXES (KWOC, INFORMATION RETRIEVAL, CURRENT AWARENESS)
The title of this section is rather long and has an unusual form, but the reason for this may soon become clear.

The 'keyword in context (KWIC) index to document titles' was first described in detail as recently as 1959 by H P Luhn[3], and by now has the status of an institution, worthy of retrospective reviews[4]. I am going to talk about indexing for KWIC (and similar) indexes which are used as systems for retrospective retrieval of information. It is worth pointing out that originally the KWIC index was seen just as an aid to rapidly produced current awareness information systems, for example the KWIC index to *Chemical titles*, the advantage of the system being timeliness[5]; it was not intended to take the place of other indexes. KWIC indexes of this type are produced from authors' titles using automatic (machine) indexing. This involves comparison of the titles, usually held on magnetic tape with a list, held in computer storage, of trivial words and other words not to be used as descriptors. The words in this so-called 'stoplist' occurring in the titles are not selected as keywords and the remaining words, now keywords, are used as the basis for the printed index. So there are no human indexing problems in producing KWIC indexes of this type.

However, KWIC indexes are also used for information retrieval, but if they are to be effective some problems appear. These problems centre upon the suitability of titles for information retrieval purposes[6] —that is, to be of any use the title must be both informative and retrievable. This involves an editing stage for most titles, either a complete rewriting of the title or the addition of suitable additional descriptors from the text of the document. This is what I have done in the title of this section, using additional words like 'information' and 'KWOC'. The title could very easily have been 'Problems of permutation indexes'—not very descriptive. Another example where the intervention of an editor is required is when features unsuitable for keypunching, like Greek symbols and chemical formulae, appear in the title. When so much editing and additional human indexing is necessary, it seems illogical to use a stoplist for selection of keywords. An example of a (fictional) title consisting entirely of words in a stop-list is *An application oriented explanation of machine models used by the aerospace companies*[7]. In the absence of editing this title would have been suppressed, although it is quite informative in this form. An example of KWIC index with edited titles is shown in figure 1, with additional terms like 'book review'.

If authors could be induced to make their titles more informative, indexing using a stoplist might become more effective for producing KWIC indexes for retrospective searching.

One drawback of the KWIC index in its normal form is the limitation placed on title length by the line-size of conventional computer print-out. At 132 characters per line only about 120 characters are left if an adequate reference to the title is included. Since descriptive titles with additional keywords may be considerably longer than 120 characters, they are often truncated and to read the whole title another keyword may have to be looked up, or as in *Chemical titles* a short coded reference directs the user to a bibliographic section where the full

LASERS AND LASER · MATERIALS. = LASERS AND LASER MATERIALS. · 65JAN MATERIAL RES3
AND ADVANTAGES OF · MAZZONI PROCESS. = COOLING, DRYING AND FURTHER PROCESSING OF SCAPS. CUTLINE AND ACVAN · 65OCT FETTE SEIFEN E3
ROL). = AUTOMATIC · MEASUREMENT OF FLOW OF SOLIDS IN A SUSPENSION. (CONTROL). = AUTCMATIC MEASUREMENT CF · 65OCT25CHEM ABSTR. 11C26
IN EUROPE. = HOT · MELT ADHESIVES IN EUROPE. = HOT MELT ADHESIVES IN EUROPE. · 65AUG ADHESIVE ACE2N
AY PATTERN. = HOT · MELT APPLIER LAYS DOWN DOT OR SPRAY PATTERN. = HOT MELT APPLIER LAYS DCWN DOT CR SPRA · 65NOV ADHESIVE ACE2
. = THEORY OF · MELTING. = THEORY OF MELTING. · 65NOV2GPHYS REV A155G
PHILICITY ON TRANS · MEMBRANE EFFLUX. = THE EFFECTS OF INCREASING NUCLEOPHILICITY CN TRANS MEMRANE EFFLUX · 65OCT INDEX MEDIC 53752
NATOMY OF THE CELL · MEMBRANE. THE PHYSICAL STATE OF WATER IN THE LIVING CELL. = PHYSIOLOGY ANC ANATOMY CF · 65OCT INDEX MEDIC S99
= SKIN SEE ALSO · MEMBRANES SEE ALSO CELL MEMBRANE SEEALSO MEMBRANE SEE ALSC PROTEIN SEE ALSC = SKI ·
= SKIN SEE ALSO · MEMBRANES SEE ALSO CELL MEMBRANE SEEALSO KERATIN SEE ALSC PROTEIN SEE ALSC = SKI ·
ODUCTION CF PCROUS · MEMBRANES FOR BATTERIES AND FUEL CELLS. = PRODUCTION OF POROUS MEMBRANES FOR BATTERIE · 65OCT25CHEM ABSTR. 1CC5G
PORTING EPITHELIAL · MEMBRANES IN VITRO. = A METHOD FCR MEASURING MICROMOLAR QUANTITIES OF CARECN CICXIDE · 65OCT INDEX MEDIC 53792
IPIDS OF BACTERIAL · MEMBRANES. = LIPIDS OF BACTERIAL MEMBRANES. · 65NOV4CHEM ABSTR. 13722
GANIZATION OF CELL · MEMBRANES. = ROLE OF WATER STRUCTURE IN THE MOLECULAR ORGANIZATION OF CELL MEMBRANES. · 65JAN CCLLCIC J. BE
ETIC PROPERTIES OF · MEMBRANES.(PERMEABILITY EVALUATION). = ISCTOPE FLOWS ANC FLUX RATIOS IN BIOLOGICAL M · 65OCT INDEX MEDIC S99
TRANSPORT AT CELL · MEMBRANES. REVIEW LECTURE. = MOLECULAR TRANSPORT AT CELL MEMBRANES. REVIEW LECTURE. · 65NOV5MELWYN BULL 22
TIOS IN BIOLOGICAL · MERCAPTANS AND B-AMINO THIOSULFATES. = THE SYNTHESIS · 65OCT11CHEM ABSTR. 3C1CC
NTHESIS OF B-AMINO · MERCAPTANS AND B-AMINO THIOSULFATES VIA ETHYLENIMINE INTERMEDIATES. = THE SYNTHESIS S · 65NOV J CRG CHEM. 36E9
STRY SEE ALSC = · MERCURY SEE ALSO ELECTROCHEMISTRY SEE ALSC = MERCURY SEE ALSC ELECTROCHEMISTRY S
ETRY SEE ALSC = · MERCURY SEE ALSO POLAROGRAPHY SEE ALSO AMALGAM SEE ALSO CHRCNOPCTENTICMETRY SEE
RUCTURES OF LIQUID · MERCURY AND LIQUID ALUMINIUM. = THE STRUCTURES OF LIQUID MERCURY ANC LIQUID ALUPINIUM · 65NOVICACTA CRYS. EC7
NCENTRATING ON THE · MERCURY DROP SURFACE. = SENSITIVITY OF THE PCLARGGRAPHIC DETERMINATION OF ANICNS AFTE · 65VOL1NZ ANAL CHEP 1C6
AN EQUILIBRIUM? · MERCURY] DROP ELECTRODE. = DIRECT DETERMINATION CF THE SURFACE EXCESS OF · 65OCT25CHEM ABSTR. 1C720
Y ADSORBED IONS ON · MERCURY. = DIRECT DETERMINATION CF THE SURFACE EXCESS OF SPECIFICALLY ADSCRBEC ICNS O · 65OCT11CHEM ABSTR. 9A55
N OF A STATIONARY! · MERCURY) DROP ELECTRODE. = CONVECTION DURING POLARIZATION OF A STATICNARY(MERCURY) C · 65NOVE6CHEM ABSTR. 12AC6
YDRATION CF SODIUM · META SILICATE. = CALORIMETRIC STUDY OF THE HYDRATION CF SODIUM META.SILICATE. · 65OCT15J CHEP PHYS 2725
SORPTION IN SODIUM · METABORATE SOLUTION. = ULTRASONIC ABSORPTION IN SODIUM METABORATE SOLUTION.
LLIC SEE ALSO = · METAL SEE ALSO ORGANOMETALLIC SEE ALSO = METAL SEE ALSC ORGANOMETALLIC SEE ALSO · 65OCT BUL SCC C19521
LLIC SEE ALSO = · METAL SEE ALSO ORGANOMETALLIC SEE ALSO = METAL SEE ALSO ORGANOMETALLIC SEE ALSO · 65OCT BUL SCC.CHIM2C15
IUM. STRUCTURE. = · METAL COMPLEXES AND CHELATES OF SOME N-SUBSTITUTED AMINCETHANOLS. 2. INVESTIGATICN IN · 65OCT INDEX MEDIC 3AC6
ANTIQUITY? · METAL COMPLEXES AND CHELATES OF SCME N-SUBSTITUED AMINCETHANCLS. 1. INVESTIGATICN IN AC · 65NOV J PHYS CHEP 3025
TYRENE MOLECULES ON · METAL COMPOUNDS. = PERCUTANEOUS TOXICITY OF METAL COMPOUNDS. · 65NOV J PHYS CHEP 623
OUBLENE AVERADBT ON · METAL OXIDE.SINGLE CRYSTALS. = ACSORPTION OF POLAR MOLECULES ON METAL OXICE SINGLE CR · 65APR PLS CHEM REV521
COVALENT ORGANO · METAL-ICLOMPOUNDS ANTHE PATH. = THE STRUCTURE OF THE ELECTRICAL DOUBLE LAYER CF THE · 65NOV MATERIALS PR95
RAYS. = MEASURING · METALLIC CORROSION BY RADIATION BACK.SCATTERING AND RADIATION INDUCED X-RAYS. = PEASUR · 65VOL1NZ ANAL CHEP 225
3. = COMPLEXES OF · METALLOCHROMIC SUBSTANCES. 10. HIGH-SENSITIVE AND SELECTIVE DETERMINATION CF CCPPER BY · 65NCV REV SCI INST155G
SILE HOT STAGE FOR · METALLOGRAPHIC EXAMINATION. = TENSILE HOT STAGE FOR METALLOGRAPHIC EXAMINATION. · 65NOV JAN PATERIAL RES30
LE FATIGUE LIFE FOR · METALS. = CORRELATION BETWEEN CYCLIC STRAIN RANGE ANC LOW-CYCLE FATIGUE LIFE CF METAL · 65NOVE.CHEM ABSTR. 12271
ION AND REMOVAL OF · METALS. = ELECTROCHEMICAL METHODS OF APPLICATION AND REMOVAL OF METALS. · 65NOV ADHESIVE ACE2N
ION OF POLYMERS TO · METALS. = HOW TEMPERATURE DEPENDENCE AND ACTIVATION ENERGY AFFECTS THE ADHESION CF AC · 65NOVE6CHEM ABSTR. 12A7E
ATHODE DEPOSITS ON · METALS. = THEORY AND PRACTICE OF USING SURFACTANTS IN SIMPLE ELECTRCLYTES TC IMPRCVE · 65OCT25CHEM ABSTR. 11729
AND VARNISHES FOR · METALS. (METHODS OF APPLICATION, CORROSION PREVENTION). (BOOK REVIEW). = PAINTS AND VARN · 65DEC J OIL CCLCR1137
S FLOW. = THERMAL · METER FOR GAS FLOW. = THERMAL METER FOR GAS FLOW. · 65OCT11CHEM ABSTR. 1CC75
ICAL STYRENE-BUTYL. · METHACRYLATE COPOLYMERS. = COMPOSITION HETEROGENEITY OF STATISTICAL STYRENE-BUTYL MET · 65OCT Z PHYSIK C· 1
= PERFLUOROALKYL · METHACRYLATE POLYMERS. WATERPROOFING OF PAPER. = PERFLUOROALKYL METHACRYLATE PCLYMERS. · 65OCT15.J CHEP PHYS 223E
ENE- STYRENE-ALKYL · METHACRYLATE TERPOLYMERS. = BUTADIENE- STYRENE-ALKYL METHACRYLATE TEPPCLYMERS. · 65NCV J PHYS CHEP 3752
WEIGHT POLY METHYL · METHACRYLATE. = VISCOSITY AND MOLECULAR WEIGHT OF LOW-MOLECULAR-WEIGHT PCLY PETHYL PE · 65NOV ANALYST. 66A
= DISSOLUTION OF · METHANE IN NICKEL FILMS. = DISSOLUTION OF PETHANE IN NICKEL FILMS.
TRUCTURE OF LIQUID · METHANE. = X-RAY DETERMINATION OF THE STRUCTURE OF LIQUID PETHANE.
S. = DIFFUSION OF · METHANE; ETHANE; PROPANE; AND N- BUTANE IN WATER FROM 25 TO 43 DEGREES. = CIFFLSION C
E DETERMINATION OF · METHANOL BY OXIDATION TO FORMALDEHYDE AND PCLAROGRAPHIC REDUCTION. (CETERMINATICN CF M

FIGURE I

title is found. The KWOC (keyword-out-of-context) index gets around this difficulty by printing the whole title with the keyword (see figure 2). We have adopted an index of this type as the basis for the information retrieval of internal documents at Port Sunlight.

RETRIEVAL FROM KWIC INDEXES: CROSS-REFERENCING AND INFORMATION RETRIEVAL THESAURI

One of the essentials in the use of printed indexes for information retrieval is that to use them efficiently a searcher must have some idea of which words or their variants may have been used in the titles he wishes to retrieve. To show how subject matter can be scattered throughout the index, take for example the term 'nuclear magnetic resonance'. This might occur as 'nuclear magnetic resonance', the slightly broader 'magnetic resonance' or the narrower term 'proton magnetic resonance': in its abbreviated form it could occur as 'NMR' or 'N.M.R.', and these terms would appear in different parts of the index.

One way of signalling these common synonyms and related terms is by the use of 'see also' cross references (see figure 1) which are printed together with the appropriate words in the index.

We have already seen how a thesaurus can be used to help in the indexing of documents, and it follows that the same thesaurus can be used to help a searcher ' to frame an enquiry appropriate to the scope and degree of his immediate interests—an enquiry employing all the terms of the retrieval vocabulary which have appropriate meaning and specificity '—Wall[8]. Using a thesaurus for indexing imposes a constraint on the indexer, who is obliged to select only terms found in the thesaurus unless there is a good case for the admission of a new term to the canon. And when new terms are admitted to the thesaurus or terms are isolated from it, corrections may have to be made to the index, often involving the reindexing of documents.

An alternative to this restrictive process is to transfer the onus of term selection from the indexer to the searcher by using a thesaurus designed primarily as a search aid. An example of a thesaurus used in searching is shown in figure 3. Briefly to describe the meanings of the relationships, GN is ' generic is ', SP is ' specific is ', SY is ' synonym ', and RT is ' related term '. These relationships do not differ from those found in indexing thesauri, but the relationship ' post on ' indicating preferred synonyms is not used in a searching thesaurus which does not seek to restrict word selection at either the indexing or searching

ADHESION

67 FEB J COLL SCI 174 — THE THEORY OF THE COAGULATION OF EMULSIONS . SMOLUCHOWSKI KINETICS SEDIMENTATION ADHESION =

ADSORPTION

66 MAY COLL J 310 — ADSORPTION AND PIGMENTATION PROPERTIES OF TITANIUM DIOXIDE WITH MODIFIED SURFACE . 1. PIGMENT RUTILE MODIFIED BY A MIXTURE OF ALUMINUM AND SILICON OXIDES BY A WET METHOD.=

66 MAY COLL J 329 — INFLUENCE OF ADSORPTION OF NONPARAMAGNETIC COMPOUNDS BY OXIDIZED AND GRAPHITIZED CARBON BLACKS ON THEIR EPR SPECTRA. BENZENE =

67 FEB J COLL SCI 188 — A COMPARISON OF MODELS FOR ELECTRIC DOUBLE LAYER . SURFACE POTENTIAL SURFACE CHARGE DENSITY INTERFACE ADSORPTION COUNTER ION COAGULATION =

ADSORPTIVE

66 MAY COLL J 271 — ADSORPTIVE INTERACTION BETWEEN SURFACE-ACTIVE SUBSTANCES AND POLYMER S. 1. WETTING OF RUBBER SURFACES BY EMULSIFIER SOLUTIONS.=

ALCOHOLS

67 FEB J COLL SCI 165 — A THEORY OF AQUEOUS EMULSIONS . 1. NEGATIVE INTERFACIAL TENSION AT THE OIL/WATER INTERFACE . SOAP ALCOHOLS FILM PRESSURE CHEMICAL POTENTIAL HYDROGEN BONDING VAN DER WAALS FORCE =

ANTISEPTIC

67 JUL TENSIDE 217 — CHANGES IN THE ANTISEPTIC PROPERTIES OF CATIONIC SURFACTANTS IN THE PRESENCE OF NONIONIC SURFACTANTS. 1. ALKYL DIMETHYL BENZYL AMMONIUM CHLORIDES AND NONYL PHENOL-ETHYLENE OXIDE ADDUCTS. QUATERNARY AMMONIUM CHLORIDE =

AQUEOUS

67 FEB J COLL SCI 165 — A THEORY OF AQUEOUS EMULSIONS . 1. NEGATIVE INTERFACIAL TENSION AT THE OIL/WATER INTERFACE . SOAP ALCOHOLS FILM PRESSURE CHEMICAL POTENTIAL HYDROGEN BONDING VAN DER WAALS FORCE =

BENZENE

66 MAY COLL J 329 — INFLUENCE OF ADSORPTION OF NONPARAMAGNETIC COMPOUNDS BY OXIDIZED AND GRAPHITIZED CARBON BLACKS ON THEIR EPR SPECTRA. BENZENE =

CARBON

66 MAY COLL J 329 — INFLUENCE OF ADSORPTION OF NONPARAMAGNETIC COMPOUNDS BY OXIDIZED AND GRAPHITIZED CARBON BLACKS ON THEIR EPR SPECTRA. BENZENE =

CATIONIC

67 JUL TENSIDE 217 — CHANGES IN THE ANTISEPTIC PROPERTIES OF CATIONIC SURFACTANTS IN THE PRESENCE OF NONIONIC SURFACTANTS. 1. ALKYL DIMETHYL BENZYL AMMONIUM CHLORIDES AND NONYL PHENOL-ETHYLENE OXIDE ADDUCTS. QUATERNARY AMMONIUM CHLORIDE =

FIGURE 2

point. The incorporation of new terms into a searching thesaurus only requires a refereeing stage to determine, for example, whether the new word is significant enough to be a keyword and to correct spelling mistakes. The new terms can then be assigned to their appropriate relationships with terms already present in the thesaurus. The size of the thesaurus is not restricted and additions to it only affect the efficiency with which subsequent enquiries are framed.

```
ULSTRON  . . . . . . . .  GN  POLYPROPYLENE

ULTRASONIC ABSORPTION  . . . .  GN  ACOUSTIC TECHNIQUE

ULTRAVIOLET SPECTRA  . . . . .  GN  MOLECULAR SPECTRA
                                RT  FLUORESCENT SPECTRA
                                SY  ELECTRONIC ABSORPTION SPECTRA

ULTRAVIOLET SPECTROPHOTOMETRY  . .  GN  MOLECULAR SPECTROSCOPY
                                    SY  UV

UNSATURATED FATTY ACID  . . .  GN  FATTY ACID
                               SP  OLEIC ACID(C18)
                               SP  RICINOLEIC ACID(C18)

UV  . . . . . . . . .  SY  ULTRAVIOLET SPECTROPHOTOMETRY

VACUUM CLEANER DUST  . . . . .  GN  SOIL

VALENCE  . . . . . . . .  GN  ATOMS
                          RT  BONDING
```

FIGURE 3

Enquirers can be helped to phrase their questions by other insertions in the thesaurus, for example by notes to indicate what conventions (if any) indexers have used in the selection of keywords or scope notes to define ambiguous terms (see figure 4).

```
BLACK SOAP FILM  . . . . . . .  GN  FILM

BLEACH  . . . . . . . .  GN  INGREDIENT

BLEACHING  . . . . . . .  GN  PRODUCT PROPERTY-IN-USE
                          RT  STAIN REMOVAL
                          RT  WHITENING

BLEACHING POWDER .  . . . . . .  GN  POWDER
                                 RT  ENZYME BLEACH
                                 RT  PRE-WASH SOAKING POWDER
                                 RT  STAIN REMOVING POWDER

BLOODSTAIN  . . . . . . .  GN  STAIN

BLOOM  . . . . . . . .  GN  DEPOSIT

BLOOMING .  . . . . . . .  RT  EFFLORESCENCE
                           DISTINGUISH BETWEEN STORAGE
                           PROPERTY AND DISHWASHING DEPOSIT
```

FIGURE 4

If a thesaurus is going to be used, the choice of which type, indexing or searching, depends entirely on the importance attached to professional input effort, the danger being that the indexing thesaurus may eventually impose as much restraint on the input as the use of a classified index.

PERFORMANCE OF PRINTED INDEXES AND FUTURE DEVELOPMENTS

Experience of printed indexes, and in fact of all natural language indexes, is short compared with classification. Figures obtained by research workers in Unilever[1] show that even an ordinary KWIC index to authors' titles used in conjunction with an alphabetic list of natural language descriptors can achieve a recall ratio of about threequarters of that for a punched card co-ordinate index. Using the KWIC index with added descriptors and a searching thesaurus, this figure for KWIC indexes should be improved.

The future of natural language indexing looks more certain if it embraces free language co-ordination searches of computer data files to achieve the recall-relevance figures of classified indexing systems, probably in conjunction with printed indexes for immediate consultation. Most of the technical, *ie* programming, difficulties of such systems have been solved and their general adoption seems only a matter of time.

REFERENCES
[1] Shaw, T N and Rothman, H (Unilever research, to be published).
[2] Engineers' Joint Council: *Thesaurus of engineering terms.* New York, 1964.
[3] Luhn, H P: 'Keyword-in-context index for technical literature (KWIC index)'. *American documentation,* 11 (4), October 1960, 288-95.
[4] Fischer, M: 'KWIC index concepts: a retrospective view'. *American documentation,* 17 (2), April 1966, 57-70.
[5] Freeman, R R & Dyson, G M: 'Development and production of *Chemical titles,* a current awareness index publication prepared with the aid of a computer'. *Journal of chemical documentation,* 3 (1), January 1963, 21-4.
[6] Herner, S: 'Effect of automated information retrieval systems on authors' (in *Automation and scientific communication: short papers contributed to the theme sessions of the 26th annual meeting of the American Documentation Institute, Chicago, 1963,* edited by H P Luhn. Washington (DC), 1963, part 1 p 101).
[7] Brandenburg, W: 'Write titles for machine index information retrieval systems'. *Ibid,* p 57.
[8] Wall, E: *Information retrieval thesauri.* New York, Engineers' Joint Council, 1962, p 1 (PB 167948).

INDEX

98